# Praise for *The Practice of Freedom*

Aikido is the martial art for the twenty-first century. It teaches you how to live in harmony with your own body and spirit, with others, and with your environment. In this book, Wendy Palmer speaks of her quest to follow the Way of Harmony in all manner of circumstances, and tells of the many valuable and practical lessons that she has learned. Every person experiences aikido in a different way, and this is an inspiring account by a sincere and dedicated practitioner of this art.

—John Stevens, author of *The Philosophy of Aikido* and
*The Essence of Aikido: Spiritual Teachings of Morihei Ueshiba*

This is a valuable book, not just because of the information that it supplies, but because of the perspective that it offers. Wendy Palmer integrates the timeless wisdom of aikido into the modern art of living well in a fast-paced and complicated world. *The Practice of Freedom* is a book to be lived, not just read.

—Judith Lasater, Ph.D, P.T., author of
*Living Your Yoga: Finding the Spiritual in Everyday Life* and
*Relax and Renew: Restful Yoga for Stressful Times*

*The Practice of Freedom* is a wonderful teaching in embodied awareness. Wendy Palmer has long experience with aikido and Buddhism, and she weaves together their timeless principles of attentiveness, openness, and compassion. This book moves the reader along toward a black belt in living.

—Joseph Goldstein, author of *Insight Meditation: The Practice of Freedom* and *Seeking the Heart of Wisdom: The Path of Insight Meditation*

Wendy Palmer's book *The Practice of Freedom* could be titled *The Practice of Virtue.* It is a wise and eloquent guide to the good life.

—George Leonard, author of *Mastery: The Keys to Success and Long-Term Fulfillment* and *The Way of Aikido: Life Lessons from An American Sensei*

# THE PRACTICE OF FREEDOM

# THE PRACTICE OF FREEDOM

Aikido Principles as a Spiritual Guide

Wendy Palmer

With a foreword by Jack Kornfield

SHAMBHALA, BOULDER 2010

Shambhala Publications, Inc.
4720 Walnut Street
Boulder, Colorado 80301
www.shambhala.com

A Rodmell Press book

Printed in the United States of America

∞ This edition is printed on acid-free paper that meets the American National Standards Institute Z39.48 Standard.
♻ Shambhala Publications makes every effort to print on recycled paper. For more information please visit www.shambhala.com.
Shambhala Publications is distributed worldwide by Penguin Random House, Inc., and its subsidiaries.

*Library of Congress Cataloging-in-Publication Data*

Palmer, Wendy.
The practice of freedom: Aikido principles as a spiritual guide /
Wendy Palmer; with a foreword by Jack Kornfield
p. cm.
Includes index.
ISBN 978-1-64547-084-7
1. Aikido—Psychological aspects. I. Title.
GV1114.35 .P356 2002
613.7'148—dc21
2001048214

| Cover and Book Design | Gopa & Ted2 |
| Cover Calligraphy | Mitsugi Saotome Shihan |
| Cover Photograph | Jan E. Watson |
| Author Photograph | Jeff Cox |

*Dedicated to Morihei Ueshiba*

Truly, once the Way is lost,

There comes then virtue;

Virtue lost, comes then compassion;

After that morality;

And when that's lost, there's etiquette,

The husk of all good faith,

The rising point of anarchy.

—*Lao Tzu, Tao Te Ching*

# CONTENTS

# FOREWORD

You hold in your hands a wise book. Wendy Palmer offers us the gracious understandings, dignity, and compassionate spirit that have grown through a lifetime dedicated to her arts. In disciplines as diverse as aikido and meditation, prison work and parenting, she shows us how we can find the wisdom that embraces both tenderness and strength.

Wendy starts honorably, with our difficulties, chaos, and struggle. She points out that our human bodies and immediate relationships are a mirror in which to learn centeredness, responsiveness, and love under pressure. She teaches us how to move from suffering and separation to nonresistance and care, and how to reconnect with the heart's basic goodness. This book is a call to discover these possibilities in ourselves.

When you hear something good in these words, a passage that rings true and inspires your spirit, remember that it is not a call to admire the author, but an invitation to practice and embody this freedom in your own life. May her teachings and your own true practice bring you a life filled with blessings.

Jack Kornfield, author of *After the Ecstasy, the Laundry:*
*How the Heart Grows Wise on the Spiritual Path*
Spirit Rock Center, Woodacre, California
November 2001

# ACKNOWLEDGMENTS

It has been a great privilege to learn by direct transmission through the lineage of Morihei Ueshiba, the founder of aikido. The notion of practice implies learning and having teachers.

I wish to thank Mitsugi Saotome Shihan for his patience, for his generosity, and for modeling power without force. His teachings are a source of strength and inspiration.

My thanks to Hiroshi Ikeda Sensei, who has taught me about friendship, loyalty, and the power of my own focused attention.

I am deeply grateful to Kevin Choate, who has helped me to open my heart, and to Nicola Geiger, for modeling joy, courage, and endurance.

George Leonard's friendship is a great gift in my life. His energy, enthusiasm, and appreciation for all our endeavors are teachings that continue to inspire me.

I am blessed to have the love and support of my children, Tiphani and Django, who, through their very presence, help me to remember how fortunate I am.

Glen Ricafrente was the first person to lend his expertise to the work of shaping this book into a clear and cohesive form.

Sylvia Partridge helped me to open my lens of perception as she kept asking me, "What do you mean by that?"

Sandy Sedgwick typed many pages of my handwritten notes into the computer with great love.

Jack Kornfield's friendship and generosity in the journey toward publication was a source of light and much needed support. He embodies the spirit of generosity and compassion that he teaches so eloquently.

Phillip Moffitt was always there and lending his time and spirit to this project.

I wish to thank Lucy Rodriguez, Alicia Rodriguez, Olga Garcia, and all the women I encountered at the Federal Correctional Institution in Dublin, California, who triggered my interest in the notion of freedom. My thanks to Tracy Thompson, M.D., who brought me into the prison, for her support and tireless service.

Janet Levine, Sue Bender, Kaz Tanahashi, and Ruth Kissane were ever-present sources of humor, confidence, and renewal.

I deeply appreciate the generous support I received from Joseph Goldstein, Judith Lasater, and John Stevens.

Many thanks go to Katherine L. Kaiser for her time, energy, and attention in copyediting this work, and to Ty Koontz, indexer extraordinaire.

It was exciting to see the design of the book come to life. Thank you, Gopa and Veetam, of Gopa and Ted2, for your creativity and artistic vision.

I am inspired by Mitsugi Saotome Shihan's calligraphy and by Jan E. Watson's photograph, which grace the cover and pages of this book.

I am grateful to Ike Lasater and all the forces, seen and unseen, that conspired to bring me together with my publishers, Linda Cogozzo and Donald Moyer. They have guided this process with an amazing combination of precision and support.

And finally, the students in my Conscious Embodiment classes and aikido classes are ultimately the reason this book has been given life. They have shaped my understanding, my questions, and my insights. The list is too long to print here, but you know who you are. Thank you so much for the tremendous influence you have had in my life and on this work.

# INTRODUCTION

Budo *is love.*

—Morihei Ueshiba

From the time I was a small child, I struggled with a feeling of being stuck. Although I was too young to comprehend the intellectual view of what life was about, I sensed a darkness behind people's smiles and gestures. In school everyone seemed to be pretending. We pretended that we were happy, pretended that we were smart: there was no place for my feelings of isolation and confusion. The catalyst for my existential feelings was my mother's illness, multiple sclerosis. She was stuck in a body that could not walk and was losing the ability to move altogether. I could see that in the face of her illness, my father and the doctors felt helpless. This made me angry and resentful. After all, they were the people in power: if they were helpless then how could I, a young girl, move forward into my life with confidence and optimism?

My mother died of complications caused by multiple sclerosis when she was forty-nine and I was twenty-one and still in college. After graduation, I came to California to visit my sister. I was going to continue on to South America, but it was 1968, and San Francisco was "flowering." I tuned in, turned on, and dropped out. My trip to South America never materialized, and I ended up staying in the San Francisco Bay Area.

Discovering aikido in 1971 was like finding an Easter egg in the grass. Friends invited me to accompany them to a class. What a delightful surprise to find a form so full of beauty and power and that addressed my existential questions! It wasn't until I was able to examine myself in the laboratory of the aikido mat that I began to see that there was something that I could actually do about my deep underlying sense of being trapped in my own existence. On the aikido mat, for the first time, I began to see that I could take responsibility for my own freedom, and cultivate my own happiness. I began teaching in 1974. It was in 1976 that George Leonard and I founded Aikido of Tamalpais in Mill Valley, California, where we continue to teach.

In 1990, Tracy Thompson, M.D., invited me to teach at the Federal Correctional Institution, a women's federal prison in Dublin, California. Dr. Thompson, who worked at the prison, was practicing aikido at our dojo. I volunteered at the prison for seven years, during which time I became the director of the Prison Integrated Health Program. I lead classes in meditation, yoga, and Consciousness Embodiment. Inmates are not allowed to study a martial art, so the aikido principles were carefully called conflict resolution or Consciousness Embodiment classes.

My work in the prison brought this question of freedom to the surface in a very direct way. It was a powerful experience to meet women from all over the world who were incarcerated for many different reasons. Perhaps I was helpful because I could relate to the experience of feeling trapped. What was most impressive was that some of them did *not* seem stuck. They had found a way to experience a sense of freedom, even in prison.

Among inmates, the terms for the world outside the prison are *the street* or *the free world*. An inmate would refer to a time or event before her incarceration as "when I was on the street" or "when I was in the free world." Each time I left the prison, I entered life "on the street," "in the free world." Ironically, it didn't seem so free. True, I felt much more appreciation for the small things: having a bathroom that I could be alone in for as long as I wished, walking outside whenever I wanted, or eating food of my choosing. But larger issues concerning my relationship with my emotions, people, time, and work made me question what degree of freedom I was really experiencing.

The practice of aikido principles offers me a way to develop a deeper awareness of behavior in adversity. They give the tools to cultivate a more compassionate approach to life. To describe its philosophy, Morihei Ueshiba, the founder of aikido, says, "Budo is love,"[1] budo meaning a martial system based on honor and virtue. I was enamored of the idea: it resonated in a place deep inside me and offered a glimpse into the possibility of freedom from fear and the freedom to love unconditionally. Perhaps the reason that aikido has held me for so many years is the deep resonance I felt when I first encountered what seemed like a magical form that held the potential of unconditional love within a martial art.

I remember a moment years ago with my teacher Saotome Sensei during a seminar. He was standing in the middle of the mat, expounding on some aspect of the practice. He extended his hand toward me, which was, in the way we practice, an invitation for me to attack him. I was already a black belt with my own school at the time and had performed this type of interaction hundreds, maybe thousands, of times.

On this particular occasion, before I could move to rise and grab his wrist, a scenario flashed through my awareness. In my vision I arose, but not with the feeling of attacking as I was trained to do, but rather with the feeling of joining with his energy. A fluid, irresistible spiral drew my body from my seated position toward his shoulder and into a forward roll. There was no sense of me attacking or Saotome Sensei throwing me: there was only a feeling of joining with something all encompassing, a feeling of unconditional love and acceptance. Then my body arose and what had flashed through my mind as a vision actually took place.

I remember feeling astounded. I had been thrown beautifully

before, and I had experienced exquisite blends, but this was way beyond beautiful or exquisite: this was the embodied experience of "*Budo* is love." In that moment, I felt an expansiveness, or liberation from the constraints of the dualities of winning and losing, self and other, and freedom and limitation. This experience taught me at a visceral level that it is possible to transform a situation of aggression into one of loving unification. The question remained, however, *How* does this alchemy take place?

This book is an exploration, based on many years of practice, of a process that responds to the question How? How do we transform our negativity into a *budo,* how do we move from "stuckness" to freedom? In aikido I found an answer to the question How?, for aikido is a *do:* a way, path, track, or trek.

The philosophy of aikido has a profound affinity with an ancient book called the Tao Te Ching (Way of the Tao), written by the Chinese mystic Lao Tzu around 1100 B.C. For me, the Way of aikido has been a path, through physical training, to enter more deeply into the Way of the Tao.

The eighty-one verses in the Tao Te Ching (or the Tao, as it is often called) describe the benefits of experiencing an enlightened state of virtue and harmony and the suffering that arises when we lose this state. Reading and rereading these verses, I began to appreciate that the path it recommends is diametrically opposed to the socialization process of today. For instance, in verse 48, Lao Tzu says,

> The student learns by daily increment.
> The Way is gained by daily loss,
> Loss upon loss until
> At last comes rest.[2]

Losing is not something that we are taught to cultivate in this society: quite the opposite. The emphasis is on gaining, winning, or having more and more things and power.

While I was working on this book I came to a point where I realized that I was unclear as to what would be the connecting thread that would tie it all together. I opened the Tao Te Ching and turned to verse 38. As I read the verse I found that it was a perfect model on which to structure the sequence of the book.

Truly, once the Way is lost,
There comes then virtue;
Virtue lost, comes then compassion;
After that morality;
And when that's lost, there's etiquette,
The husk of all good faith,
The rising point of anarchy.[3]

I recognized anarchy as the starting position of my life and the lives of those around me. The sequence of etiquette followed by morality, compassion, and virtue reflected my own experiences of life.

I feel very fortunate to have found aikido, which has been the core of my spiritual practice. I have found the body to be the most revealing and rewarding focal point for exploring the ecumenical nature of the spiritual path, for it is through the body that an individual manifests the ideas or inspirations of this path. I can truly say that where I once felt deeply unhappy—trapped, full of self-hatred, and constantly wishing for the circumstances of my life to be different from what they were—now I have much more ease and acceptance of myself and my life. I am happier and, I think, more helpful, than I have ever been before.

Although the philosophy of aikido is suitable for all aspects of life, the vigorous quality of the physical practice is not. In order to make the principles available to more people, I developed a way of training with these principles called Conscious Embodiment. Conscious Embodiment is a form that allows aikido principles to be applied to everyday psychological and emotional situations without strenuous physical demands. This form has allowed me to study some moments that arise on the aikido mat more slowly and carefully. These two works inform each other in a way that enriches my perspective of the entire process.

Aikido's vision of unconditional love under pressure is an exciting possibility. To feel this love in the face of danger is a powerfully freeing experience. The turning of the millennium is a surge, sweeping us forward toward a new page in our history. Like many people, I sense that there is a trend toward the re-emergence of the spiritual and the soulful aspects of our lives on this planet. Is the freedom that can be found from living a virtuous and harmonious life merely a fantasy preserved in ancient texts, or is it a genuine possibility? I believe that the inquiry, the ability of a person to penetrate more deeply into his or her essential nature, is the first step in actually discovering this freedom.

## A WORD ABOUT AIKIDO

Aikido is a Japanese martial art that was given its formal name around 1940. *Aikido* can be loosely translated as "a way of harmonizing with nature (life)." It was conceived and developed by Morihei Ueshiba, born in 1883. As a young man, he was proficient in the martial arts of his time. He was a jujitsu specialist, and he also practiced sumo wrestling, sword fighting, and spear fighting. At a time when martial arts competitions frequently resulted in serious injury or death, he challenged and fought renowned martial artists throughout Japan and won all his matches.

Although he became an invincible martial artist, he was not satisfied with his development and continued his search for spiritual perfection. In his forties, he was transformed by a divine vision. After a match with a high-ranking sword fighter, which Morihei won without using a sword or touching the man, he went to his garden to wash himself with water from the well. John Stevens describes what happened next:

"The ground beneath his feet began to shake, and he was bathed with rays of pure light streaming down from heaven. A golden mist engulfed his body, causing his petty conceit to vanish, and he himself assumed the form of a Golden Being."[4] After this experience of enlightenment, Morihei focused on aikido as a spiritual path. As he says, "Aiki is not a technique to fight with or defeat the enemy. It is a way to reconcile the world and make human beings one family."[5]

Those of us who practice the art always refer to Morihei as O'Sensei, *O* meaning "great" and *sensei* meaning "teacher." It is an honorific referring only to this man: all other aikido teachers are referred to simply as Sensei. Aikido combines a philosophy of nonviolence with a spiritual base of universal divinity through unity. Its goals are self-control, compassion, and a cultivation of virtue in the art of living. The study of the art happens on three levels: the physical, the psychological, and the spiritual. These three elements are unified through something we call *ki*. As Saotome Sensei describes it, "*[Ki]* is the activity of life. . . . It is the vital essence of the universe, the creative energy of God. . . . The word *ki* can indicate a flow of energy, a vibration, an atmosphere. It can describe a state of mind, a state of health, the activity of life, the existence of spirit, or the pulsating movement of the soul."[6]

The terms *centering* and *blending* are familiar to most aikido students. *Centering* refers to a quality of physical stability that is poised and relaxed. *Blending* is the ability to go with a movement; it implies a harmonious connection, such as is experienced in partner dancing. I also use the term *opening* to describe an expansive, radiant capacity inherent in each of us. These qualities are practiced along with the form of aikido and provide a way of being that we can use in our daily lives.

There are no matches or competitions in aikido. O'Sensei says, "It is not for correcting others; it is for correcting your own mind."[7] Aikido aims at self-cultivation rather than dominating the other person. Because of this, when we practice, the one who attacks is thrown, and there is no sense of defeat in this; in fact, being thrown becomes an art form known as *ukemi*, the art of falling.

Through aikido practice, we can observe and experience the content of our responses that arise as we practice. The aikido dojo, or place of training, is a laboratory where we can experiment with the potentialities of compassion while under the physical pressure of a simulated attack. The body begins to take the form of a container through which the properties of *ki* unify the system until it becomes a conduit that delivers an assortment of universal expressions. Through committed practice and self-cultivation, we can affect the quality of the content and expression in our containers. We can open ourselves and become flexible, fluid, creative, and compassionate.

Most people come to practice the art in order to learn to function more safely, smoothly, or easily in their lives. An underlying assumption is that maturity in the practice will allow aikido students a greater sense of freedom in how they move through their lives, and that they will be able to handle attacks, real or metaphorical, without injuring others or being injured themselves. With continued practice, the deeper spiritual qualities embedded in the process find ways to raise the power of compassion in the face of aggression.

For me, aikido is a lifelong path of self-cultivation. It is a study of my physical, physiological, and spiritual limitations and potentials. Learning how to synchronize the body with itself, the mind with the body, and the spirit with the mind is no easy task. As a study of freedom, it has both sides of the issue: it is, at times, freedom *from*—from tension, fear, and aggression; it is also freedom *to*—to be open, to accept, to redirect.

春風以接人
秋霜以自肅

*part one*

INITIAL STAGES

*chapter one*

# ANARCHY

*I would like to beg you . . . to have patience with everything unre-*
*solved in your heart and try to love* the questions themselves *as if*
*they were locked rooms or books written in a very foreign language.*
*Don't search for the answers, which could not be given to you now,*
*because you would not be able to live them. And the point is, to live*
*everything.* Live the questions now. *Perhaps then, someday far in the*
*future, you will gradually, without even noticing it, live your way*
*into the answer.*

—Rainer Maria Rilke, *Letters to a Young Poet*

## AN EARLY SENSE OF ANARCHY

Anarchy began early in my life. My mother had multiple sclerosis,
and around age five I knew, in the way that a five-year old knows, that
there was, as *The American Heritage Dictionary* (second college edition) defines *anarchy,* an "absence of any cohering principle."[1] My
mother's illness made no cognitive sense, and I knew that the grown-
ups, the people of power and authority, had no grasp of it either. As
a child I resented that the "big people," who should know what to do,
were unable to keep the disease from spreading through her body.
Even the best specialists could not help her. Somehow I felt that I
couldn't trust the adults. Who, I wondered, was running the show

anyway? Life seemed unfair, unpredictable, and dangerous. I sensed that I was going to have to take care of myself and possibly my mother.

For a young child to believe that the world is not a safe place is a heavy realization. My way of dealing with this realization was to retreat into a world of horses and horse fantasy. Every day after school I would go to the stables and ride until dinnertime. When I came home from riding, I would fantasize about a land full of beautiful, intelligent horses. In this land, horses and people understood and helped each other. Relationships were based on honesty, compassion, and trust instead of helplessness and pretending.

## PUSHING THE BOUNDARIES

As I grew older, I began to push the boundaries of acceptable behavior. If I was told not to do something because it was dangerous, I would retort, "So what? We're all just going to get sick and die anyway!" And I would do whatever I wished, heedless of the danger. I think that I was trying to find out if there was any point or meaning to life as well as to irritate the adults. I wondered why everyone was speeding here and there, pretending that they were happy and that the things they were doing were important or would make any difference in the end. Most people, it seemed, weren't really happy. I thought that they were really more nervous and anxious than they were letting on, and that, I guessed, was why they drank so much. And what about death? Why did no one like to talk about death?

I had heard my mother say, at night, that she wanted to die. My grandmother died when I was four, and my grandfather when I was ten. It was obvious to me that there was no way out of this dilemma. I saw no models of self-disciplined, happy people. I derived a little enjoyment from irritating the adults; I could usually upset them by talking about death. In retrospect, I think that I insisted on talking about death because the adults' ineffectualness in the face of death threatened me. So the stage was set for me to form a negative attitude toward life.

I was not alone in my early experience of an anarchical world, but, like many disillusioned young people, I felt alone. A further paradox to this was that, although I felt alone, I also felt pressured to be a certain way and to do certain things in a social context. I resented that and I wanted to be left alone. Although, like all of us, I desperately wanted to be loved and to feel connected and secure, I simply could not bring myself to trust people. Did a Higher Power to whom I could turn exist? If a Higher Power did exist, and I suspected that it did, I was mad at it for making my mother ill.

This was my starting place. Because of the circumstances and my temperament, I felt trapped, stuck in this life. It was a place far from happiness, far from freedom.

## SEPARATION FROM UNCONDITIONAL LOVE

Many years later, when I began volunteering in the Prison Integrated Health Program at the Federal Correctional Institution, a women's prison in Dublin, California, I saw quite a few versions of my existential dilemma. I saw that many people, no matter what their color or country of origin, experience the same angst, or feelings of separation from unconditional love. Sometimes the anxiety created by this separation hardens a person, and makes a person bitter and resentful or fearful and manipulative. In my years working with many people, including prisoners, I saw many variations on this theme, but fundamentally they all seemed to stem from the same experience.

Often parents or caretakers are not aware that their own fears and frustrations are interpreted by their children as rejection. Children are dependent on adults for their sense of well-being. When adults lose their sense of well-being, the child often becomes angry or frightened. Many stories of failure and unhappiness begin with feelings of injustice and betrayal within the family structure. When a child's world begins to lose coherence, he or she either creates a different context in which things do make sense or continues to resent a world in which things do not.

It is in this context, a loss of coherence, that I use the term *anarchy*. The word *anarchy* referred to in the Tao Te Ching means "chaos," a type of deterioration rising from a base of frustration. This element is intrinsic to the process of personal growth, for without the energy of the frustration, we might never have any incentive for growth and change. Anarchy is like compost. Compost enriches the soil, so that plants can grow. Anarchy and its accompanying sensations—restlessness and frustration—provide the fuel to move us forward in our quest for freedom and happiness.

## TRAPPED AND IMPRISONED

Albert Einstein articulates the very human dilemma of feeling trapped, feeling imprisoned by life:

> A human being is a part of the whole that we call the universe, a part limited in time and space. He experiences himself, his thoughts and feelings, as something separated from the rest—a kind of optical illusion of his consciousness. This illusion is a prison for us, restricting us to our personal desires and to affection for only the few people nearest us. Our task must be to free ourselves from this prison by widening our circle of compassion to embrace all living beings and all of nature.[2]

Many people feel trapped or imprisoned by their lives. This sense of restriction is usually associated with what seems to be outer circumstances. There is often a feeling that this has been happening for a long time, since early childhood, and that we are just a link in a chain of people and events. If we are not careful, we will cultivate an identity of victim. The "victim habit" sets up an energy pattern, or vortex, such that we keep being victimized. The same kinds of things continue to happen to us. The more our minds think this way, the stronger the energy pattern becomes. Repetitive thoughts, such as, *It's just not fair, It doesn't make sense,* or *Why me?* arise. Many people turn to psychotherapy or antidepressants to try to find relief from the weight of this seemingly relentless thought pattern.

## STAYING POSITIVE IN THE FACE OF DIFFICULTIES

It has always been interesting to me that some people can have extremely difficult lives and not become depressed. How is it that they are able to function in an upbeat way in the midst of personal disaster? What is it that allows them to keep a connection to a sense of coherence, when others experience a kind of emotional anarchy— a sense of alienation—in the face of life's challenges?

I am impressed and inspired by women who have been in prison for many years who do not have a victim mentality. They use their energy to continue to educate themselves, learn new crafts, and help less centered or more fearful inmates. They don't ignore their own situation. They work on their cases, talking regularly to their lawyers, or writing letters that could help their cases. They don't whine or talk bitterly about their situation. They smile and appreciate what is positive around them. They seem to echo Anne Frank's words: "It's really a wonder that I haven't dropped all my ideals, because they seem so absurd and impossible to carry out. Yet I keep them, because in spite of everything I still believe that people are really good at heart."[3]

It is not that they don't have difficulties: they do. What seems to be the difference between these women and the bitter, angry ones is that they don't feel stuck. When they have problems, they explore ways to deal with them. They seem to have a more expansive and flexible attitude toward their dilemmas. Instead of looking for an escape, they look into the situation.

I know people with physical disabilities who have progressed in aikido up to the rank of brown belt or black belt. For example, a student who trained in our dojo for many years is a survivor of polio. Although the bones of his left hand and foot are fused together, I was continually amazed at the creative ways that he adapted his physical circumstance to each technique. He has learned to roll differently on each side. In order to accommodate the lack of mobility on his left side, he rolls while bending the knee that we usually straighten. Rather than feeling trapped or stuck by his limitations, he always looked for different ways to work with them.

## EXPERIENCING RESISTANCE

It seems that the feeling of being caught or trapped is primarily the experience of what one aikido teacher calls the physical mind: the mind of the intellect or acquired knowledge. When the physical mind feels that it can't get an answer or make sense of something, it has a tendency to tighten up. As soon as we tighten up in our minds, our bodies follow suit. The mind affects the body and vice versa. Is it possible that the feeling of freedom is more of a mental experience than a physical one? If my mind feels open and interested, then I feel free. If my mind feels tight and confused, I feel trapped.

Aikido and Conscious Embodiment have provided me with a way to study this important but difficult experience. There are times when I find that I am stuck, unable to complete the technique that was demonstrated, or, for that matter, any technique. Anger and frustration rise up in me. Sometimes they come up quickly, seemingly without a thought, and before I know it, I am tense and struggling with my partner. At other times, my frustration builds up slowly. I am more aware and I can even tell myself, *Relax, don't fight,* and yet I can still feel my muscles tightening. It is a primitive response, deeply buried in my survival instinct. I have had to learn to accept that this is me fighting the situation and not just the other person being difficult.

Rarely is it possible to study and work directly with the energy of frustration in a supportive environment. Aikido and Conscious Embodiment provide a space for this exploration. Until we come to terms with these resistant parts of ourselves, we will never be able to move on to the next stage of our processes. Our energies will be used to suppress these aggressive responses rather than integrating them.

## PAIN

Women who have experienced the labor of childbirth know that pain is part of bringing a life into the world. Pain seems to have an intrinsic place in my life. Throughout the years it has been a point of orientation, an enemy—and a friend. Different types of pain—physical pain, mental pain, emotional pain, and spiritual pain—provide familiar colors and textures in my life. Aikido is a martial art, so at times its practitioners experience physical pain. In my experience, however, the pain that is the most intense is ego pain. I feel ego pain when my image of who I am doesn't match what actually happens when I am practicing. When my image and my actions don't match up, I criticize myself with words such as *stupid, weak, wimp,* or *incompetent.* This is a very painful experience.

## ACCEPTANCE OF LIMITATIONS

When I face the truth that I am not able to do what I thought that I could do, I can begin to accept my limitations without harsh criticism. This acceptance allows me to see that what I can't do yet is what I can work toward doing. Finding my limitations helps me to know where the focus of my practice should be. In this way, my pain leads me toward freedom. Conscious Embodiment classes, which use the principles of aikido to study the self, are not physically demanding (although a practitioner needs to be able to walk), so physical pain is not an issue. Instead, my realization that my responses to relationships are often ways that I create distressing experiences for myself is painful. Experiencing my patterns in relationship is where I meet my training edge.

The first of the Four Noble Truths taught by the Buddha is "All is suffering!" Strong language, but I agree with his perspective. The pain of wanting things to be different than they are seems to be the impetus for most activity, mental as well as physical, that we perform during the day.

One of the women in prison told me that the worst time for her was just before her arrest. Her mind kept looping in a thought pattern that went something like, *Oh, God, what if they come get me? Book me? Lock me up in prison? What if they take me away from all that I know and love and trust? I am so afraid. I can't stand it: the shame is too much. I just want to close my eyes and make it go away.* This is the pain that arises from anticipation. Her pain and fear were triggered by the thought of losing what was familiar. The fear of being abandoned and the fear of being intruded upon physically and emotionally are extremely difficult for anyone to handle. These kinds of pain are the result of thought forms. The actual loss may be different from the anticipated loss. In the moment of actual loss, we experience pain because we compare our not having something to a time when we did have that something. These comparing thoughts trigger feelings, and our pain becomes emotional as well as mental.

## EMOTIONAL PAIN

Many books and songs are about emotional or spiritual pain. The pain is often described in terms of loss or longing. The blues is a style of music based on pain: the pain of lost love, the pain of jilted love, and the pain of unrequited love. Somehow the music encourages the listener to enjoy these feelings. From this perspective, emotional pain has a certain popularity because it resonates so easily with what is in many people's hearts.

Pain can bring people together in the effort to overcome it. It is the orientation point for most of the Alcoholics Anonymous, Narcotics Anonymous, and other twelve-step groups. Psychologists and psychiatrists make their living by listening to people talk about their pain.

## PHYSICAL PAIN

Pain that has a seemingly physical orientation is interesting to study. Say that I stub my toe or scrape my finger. These events can seem separate or disassociated from the process that I thought that I was involved in: that is, while walking across the room to get a book, I stubbed my toe. But they can also be seen as punctuations of the process. These interruptions are reminders of how vulnerable I am in my casing of flesh and bones. Reminders of the potential for pain can arise at any moment, reminders that I am not completely in control of myself or my environment.

I began to appreciate physical pain during ten-day silent meditation retreats. Although mental and emotional pain arise from past or future events, physical pain is often about the present. Physical pain hurts in the body and it hurts now. Usually, I had pain in my knees or back. The pain was unpleasant, but it gave me something compelling and tangible to focus on in the present moment. It wasn't until I experienced an hour of sitting without pain that I realized how the pain had kept me in the present. Without pain, my mind wandered away into fantasies and judgments, rarely returning to the present and my body. Through self-cultivation, I have learned to stay more present in the moment, in my body, without the pain.

## CHRONIC PAIN

Usually when we speak of chronic pain, we are talking about physical pain. Typically, chronic back pain means that a person's back hurts most of the time, regardless of any amount of painkillers. As the Buddha points out, we are all in chronic pain and continuously struggle with some amount of angst or dissatisfaction. The notion of pain-killers is typical of the Western cultural view: what we are uncomfortable with, we try to kill. The more extreme version of this is the "kill for peace" mentality, which can be found in self-righteous individuals, some of whom are military leaders or government officials.

Chronic pain, pain that cannot be killed or numbed, demands attention. It sends us a clear message that something is not right. When Western medicine cannot find a way to stop or cure the pain, a person may turn to alternative therapies, such as visualization, meditation, bodywork, or talk therapy. This is, in a sense, a search for liberation: freedom from pain seems to be the main concern. Because modern drugs don't usually hold the answers—they only moderate or suppress the symptoms—the question that should be asked is, Where does the pain come from? What is its origin? Is the person being tortured by an outside force over which he or she has no control, or does the torture come from within, a product of the person's mind and imagination?

## PAIN OF SEPARATION AND ISOLATION

There is the sense of the pain of separation from our original connection with divine intelligence or oneness. It's the "fall from grace," the archetypal story of being cast out of the Garden of Eden. This pain of separation is made more intense by the possibility of connection.

Isolation implies the even more frightening possibility of annihilation. The shadow of shame causes contraction and fear, driving us further from the warmth of love and acceptance. Envy, which springs from the notion that others are still wandering happily in the garden, creates resentment and self-hatred. For some, their experience of these dark corners of the inner life is excruciating, and they use drugs, food, or entertainment in an attempt to numb the pain. Their task is to stay ahead of the pain.

## FACING AND ACCEPTING OUR PAIN

Our standards for happiness become diluted in the anarchy of pain, and we settle for simply finding ways to try to escape pain. This is the desire for freedom from the pain of isolation. It is, unless we face and examine its origin, what drives our lives. A form of self-cultivation that focuses on openness and stability can help us recover a loving relationship with the universe.

Pain, for better or worse, is part of our lives. As unpleasant as pain is, important information can be gleaned from it. The compost metaphor applies to pain as well as to the frustration that accompanies anarchy. Even if it is packaged in a brightly colored plastic bag, it is still manure or food that has rotted. Despite its humble origin, compost enriches the soil, helping to produce healthy plants. In the same way, our pain can be a valuable way to enrich the soul by increasing our compassion.

Pema Chödrön, an inspiring Buddhist teacher, is clear about the necessity of working with pain: "Only to the degree that we've gotten to know our personal pain, only to the degree that we've related with pain at all, will we be fearless enough, brave enough, and enough of a warrior to be willing to feel the pain of others."[4] In this way, our emotional pain has, at last, found a purpose: it can be used to fertilize our capacity for compassion. In order to do this, the pain must be worked with, not rejected.

## IMPOVERISHMENT VERSUS THE LARGER VIEW

*The American Heritage Dictionary* (second college edition), defines *impoverish* as follows: "To reduce to poverty; make poor; to deprive of natural richness or strength."[5]

In aikido, impoverishment often shows up as a narrowing of focus. Suddenly, the world becomes my partner's arm, and I don't have the power to make it do what I want. When this syndrome surfaces, I have watched myself and others become tight. Usually, it feels as though there is not enough room or energy to execute the technique. It is an old, familiar, painful feeling of "not enough": not having enough or not being enough. The aikido mat is a place where this situation can be studied and, little by little, I came to understand that I am doing this to myself. It is *my* tightness, not my partner's, that makes the technique so difficult.

This sense of poverty occurs when we look at others and compare ourselves with them. In this regard, advertisements have an extraordinarily powerful effect on the subconscious. We are constantly receiving messages that if we buy this or drink that or go here or there, then we will become happy and healthy, and stay forever young. Yet if you look closely into the lives of many people who actually have or do those things, you will see that they are not particularly happy. One of the powerful teachings of the O. J. Simpson murder trial is that, even though he had fame, fortune, and good looks, he was not a happy person. He, too, experienced a kind of impoverishment: he was not content. As is often the case, something was missing. The missing thing is usually sought in the external world, and it annoys and unsettles us, making it hard for us to quiet down and see the bigger picture.

We can learn to acknowledge impoverished thoughts and then move on to take the larger view. Life is full of ebbs and flows: breath goes in and out, and night follows day. Things come and then go, are hard and then easy, are hot and then cold, or are up and then down. This is natural: it happens throughout the world to everyone, everywhere. Yet in most cases, we think that it is being done to us. We may feel that it is not fair, that someone else wins the lottery and we do not. We may think that other people are happier because they have more money, or because they are taller or thinner or younger.

A few years ago, I read about a woman named Peace Pilgrim. She had spent many years walking across the United States, with only the clothes she was wearing, a toothbrush, and one or two inspiring notes about peace. She told people that she was on a pilgrimage to spread the words and feelings of peace. On the material plane, she had nothing, and looking at her from a purely physical point of view, a person might say that she was impoverished. But when I read about her, I realized that she was one of the richest people in the world. She was happy and fearless. She loved all things and, in turn, was loved by them. Her life was filled with joy, and her example nurtured those she encountered on her journey.

## ACHIEVEMENT AS A SABOTAGE PATTERN

Most of our culture is organized around material gain and achievement: the more things that we have, is the implicit message, the happier we will be. Credentials are also in the category of things that imply that we are special—worthy of respect, affection, and admiration—and that this specialness should make us happier. What we don't realize is that we are in the habit of feeling that if only this or that would happen, then we could be happy. And yet, if we suddenly got what we wanted, it might be a little scary. We could have a crisis of identity: we would have to see ourselves in a different light. We would no longer yearn for power, love, and respect: we would have it.

This is an important moment to examine, for the euphoria of sudden achievement is often followed by a letdown of equal magnitude. Extreme highs are followed by extreme lows. A sabotage pattern may become apparent. If dissatisfactions had been a habit, then a person may continue to tell himself or herself the same type of negative things: *I never get to have what I want, I never get to keep what I have gotten, and Things are always being taken from me.* In order to break this habit, an individual needs to really see how the mind keeps fixating on these thought patterns. It takes an effort to stop and observe the mind with some detachment, but if a person is willing to make the effort, the situation can be seen from another perspective. He or she can look at it from the outside: step back, get a little distance, and observe it from an aerial or panoramic view.

Impoverishment breeds resentment. Resentment grows because of comparison: *I resent others because they have more than I do.* If the energy of these thoughts keeps building, then aggressive feelings emerge. If these feelings grow strong enough, then they become rage. Rage leads to self-destructive behavior, creating confusion and chaos. This is the territory of anarchy. It is fueled by frustration and resentment. It involves a struggle within the self, between the part that wants to be free from neediness and the part that wants to satisfy the desire for fulfillment with more things, people, and experiences.

This sense of frustration or conflict is a sign of life, an urge toward freedom. As this energy wells up, it needs some way to organize itself. Energy needs boundaries and a reference point if it is to be a positive, creative force. Socially, these boundaries or forms could be defined as etiquette. Etiquette gives some feeling of cohesion and order to the awakening of vitality and the desire for freedom.

*chapter two*

# ETIQUETTE

*The purpose of etiquette . . . is self-defense.*

    —Katsuyuki Kondo Sensei, quoted in *Aikido Journal*

## ETIQUETTE AS FORM

Studying the expression of greetings is an interesting way to study etiquette. As a young girl, I was shown that you shake hands with some people, hug and kiss others, and nod and smile when you are uncertain. When I was in Europe, I was kissed on both cheeks and, on occasion, had my hand kissed by way of greeting. I found that some of these forms were easier to adjust to than others.

Interestingly enough, when I began studying aikido, the forms of greeting within the art, which almost always involve bowing, seemed easy and familiar to me. The bow is a greeting that implies respect. Somehow, this was easier for my system to grasp than the kiss, which seems to be more of a statement of intimacy or affection. When entering an aikido dojo, we bow. That is, we greet the room with respect. When we step onto the actual training surface, the mat, we bow again. We bow to our teacher and training partners; they bow in return. Physical touch is not part of the interaction, yet I often feel truly connected with the people and the environment when observing this form of etiquette. There is a kind of spaciousness that allows me to feel the nuances and subtleties of the situation.

## MAAI

Stanley Pranin, editor in chief of *Aikido Journal,* has an interesting way of comparing the social space of etiquette with the martial arts concept of *maai. Maai* is the distance, or combative interval, between two opponents. Understanding and maintaining the correct *maai* has much to do with the outcome of the exchange. Historically speaking, failure to adopt the correct *maai* has resulted in injury or death. As Pranin writes,

> Through the forms of etiquette, the metaphorical maai of all concerned parties is defined and maintained during the course of their interaction. A safe distance is achieved, thus leading to a predictable outcome: the preservation of social order. A lapse in the observance of the expected behavior produces a shift in this psychological spacing. One party finds his space violated and feels the need to take retaliatory measures. The threatened person may then bring to bear the powers of sanction of the group to punish the violator.
>
> Viewed this way, etiquette is closely related to the notion of territoriality in a behavioral context.
>
> Gradually with the passage of time, customs and manners change to reflect the shifting values of a society.[1]

## SOCIAL ETIQUETTE

Etiquette is a form that shapes us socially. Form, in the case of behavior, is the container that shapes and informs our actions and our attitudes. Form is a container through which inspiration can be expressed in a useful way. We compose songs, we write books, we draw pictures, and we create sculptures, all within an acceptable social format. Without form, social interactions would be confusing, chaotic, and dangerous. Form can also been seen as a map that helps us to locate ourselves. We can find our position, and we can change our position based on our knowledge of the map, which shows the locations of people and events. Social etiquette is the map for living according to the social regulations of the time.

Throughout the history of socialized humanity there has been social etiquette; this was originally based on the survival of the group. The form was dictated by the leaders of the group, whose authority created cohesion by demanding submission, which allowed each member to be assured of a place in the whole. Throughout time, the leaders began to refine their organizational skills and institutions developed. With the birth of democracy, agreement was substituted for dominance. The forms, which were once based on survival and held in place by force, were now arrived at by agreement. These agreements became moral and ethical codes that directed and organized the rules of behavior in terms of right and wrong. Modern morality was inspired by new ideas and possibilities, possibilities that included such lofty ideals as honesty, virtue, and the right to life, liberty, and the pursuit of happiness.

Social etiquette limits some behavior and encourages, if not demands, others. In the social hierarchy, there are those who serve and those who are served. Whether a person serves by demand or by choice is the difference between etiquette and morality. In some cases, the service may stem from a suggestion; in others, a requirement. Either way, the form is imposed from without, and there is a strong emphasis on appearance. However, if the form begins to resonate with the ring of truth within the people who serve as a vital force, then it crosses over into the territory of morality.

## SAMURAI ETIQUETTE

For the sixteenth-century samurai of Japan, the sole purpose of all action was to serve and protect his lord. Etiquette dictated that a samurai was not permitted to touch money; the issues of material gain that so plague us today were not relevant to him. Instead, martial valor was the goal of his life, which was one of constant training. His attitude was one of acceptance of and obedience to the commands of his lord. Even to commit *seppuku,* or ritual suicide, he had to have permission from his lord, the only exception being if the lord himself was dead. If the samurai loved and respected his lord, then his moral motivation made his self-sacrificing behavior a fulfilling and unwavering path. The Japanese art of aikido has ancestral roots in the samurai mentality. The respect we show for the founder, our teachers, and our training partners begins as etiquette and develops into moral commitment.

A road map tells us where to go and the distance between the cities that we will encounter along the way. But once we have actually driven the road, we have a more visceral feeling for the names of places and the terrain the next time that we look at the map. Similarly, it is not until we commit ourselves to the practice, or form, of etiquette that we can make a fair judgment as to whether we wish to deepen our commitment to that behavior. When forms are cultivated and developed in some way, they become powerful tools for manifesting modes of behavior. It is helpful and important to understand that what is cultivated becomes strong. We get good at what we do again and again.

In order for behavior to be moral, there has to be an emotional or heartfelt relationship to the actions. My commitment to O'Sensei's vision of unconditional love has deepened throughout time. I am fortunate to be able to see and feel the powerful and compassionate technique of my teachers Saotome Sensei and Hiroshi Ikeda Sensei. They inspire me to deepen my practice. The form we use allows us to discover our unique expression of each technique. The principles, which emerge from the creative process, vitalize the form. The form contains and organizes the principles. In this way, etiquette is an intrinsic part of the organizing principle.

## EVOLUTION

J. Krishnamurti says the following about evolution, or personal growth: "We ask ourselves is it possible to break through this heavy conditioning of centuries immediately and not enter into another conditioning—to be free, so that the mind can be altogether new, sensitive, alive, aware, intense, capable?"[2]

Somehow there is a process, a journey, that must be undertaken, a type of etiquette or map that must be in place in order to evolve, in order to proceed in our lives. Life seems to have an evolution in which we develop and learn and, it is to be hoped, become mature, kind, and creative people. Otherwise, we live out our shadow side, using people and things to try to protect ourselves from the fear and responsibility of our lives and individuality. One of the questions that I keep asking myself is, *Do I have the power, the spirit, to choose the path of kindness and creativity?*

Eric Fromm says the following about personal evolution:

> We see that the process of growing human freedom has the same dialectic character that we have noticed in the process of individual growth. On the one hand it is a process of growing strength and integration, mastery of nature, growing power of human reason, and growing solidarity with other human beings. But on the other hand this growing individuation means growing isolation, insecurity, and thereby growing doubt concerning one's own role in the universe, the meaning of one's life, and with all that a growing feeling of one's own powerlessness and insignificance as an individual.[3]

## LEARNING TO FALL

In aikido, half of the practice is learning to be thrown and to fall. During training, one person attacks, is thrown, and falls four times.

Then the roles are reversed, and the other person falls four times. Learning to fall is not only a useful skill for maintaining our safety: it is an art form unto itself. When we fall, the fall is an opportunity to accept change and come back to standing again without incurring any damage. Instead of viewing a fall as a defeat or loss, we fall willingly. Because we fall willingly, there is a grace and an ease in the movement. This is what makes it possible for falling to be an art form.

In rolling, we practice form. The form gives stability to the situation. Just as etiquette organizes and stabilizes society, so the form of falling in aikido, called *ueki,* helps us to organize the energy of the fall so that we are not injured. Because there is no competition in aikido, there is no loss or failure in the fall: instead, there is an appreciation of ability. We can have a positive experience from falling instead of a negative one. Instead of the fear of falling, we experience the joy of *ueki.*

Falling need not be associated with failing. Yet we can sustain such an open, spontaneous attitude only if we have an innate confidence that our place in the world is valid. So how is it that an experience of validation occurs? Through practice we can learn that wherever we find ourselves, up or down, the place has meaning and integrity.


## HISTORICAL ETIQUETTE

We have seen that we need some form and that, at times, etiquette can provide a map in approaching a situation. As Eric Fromm says, historically, until the Renaissance and the Protestant Reformation, people's social positions were fixed:

> A man had little chance to move socially from one class to another. . . . With few exceptions he had to stay where he was born. He was often not even free to dress as he pleased or to eat what he liked. . . . Personal, economic, and social life was dominated by rules and obligations from which practically no sphere of activity was exempted.[4]

In medieval times, the church provided most of the form through which a person experienced how he or she fit into the world. Individualism was discouraged, as was freedom of thought. In a wonderful passage from Dostoyevsky's *Brothers Karamazov*, the Inquisitor describes the human wish to be controlled by the church:

> Thou wouldst go into the world, and art going with empty hands, with some promise of freedom which men in their simplicity and their natural unruliness cannot even understand, which they fear and dread—for nothing has ever been more insupportable for a man and a human society than freedom.[5]

He continues,

> I tell Thee that man is tormented by no greater anxiety than to find some one quickly to whom he can hand over that gift of freedom with which the ill-fated creature is born. But only one who can appease their conscience can take over their freedom. . . . Didst Thou forget that man prefers peace, and even death, to freedom of choice in the knowledge of good and evil? Nothing is more seductive for a man than his freedom of conscience, but nothing is a greater cause of suffering.[6]

Since the establishment of democracy, individual responsibility and freedom have been encouraged. However, it is not easy for us to accept responsibility for ourselves. On the one hand, we want to be taken care of; on the other hand, we wish to be free. The cultivation of confidence and compassion can help us to integrate within ourselves these two forces with which we struggle. Etiquette is the form that holds and shapes confidence and compassion in their formative stages.

## CONTEMPORARY ETIQUETTE

The notion of humans as unique individuals is a fairly recent concept, compared with the long history of the notion of humans as tribe members whose main focus was physical survival. The Renaissance, the Protestant Reformation, and the beginning of capitalism sparked a change in outlook. Now, instead of a few dictating moral codes to the masses, each individual has the opportunity to grow beyond prescribed behavior and discover intrinsic meaning for himself or herself. Now individuals are free to make decisions about how they want to live.

But are we really? Compared with the Middle Ages, yes, we are quite free to make changes in our lives. Yet how often do we hear that so-and-so is undergoing a midlife crisis, that he is trying to figure out who he is and what he should be doing? True, we have more freedom than ever before to choose how we want to worship, but for many, faith itself is questionable. Many of us believe in something, but not in a deeply satisfying way that serves as a moral compass that can direct our lives. True, we also have, at least in certain countries, freedom of speech, but how many of us can formulate an original idea? I would say that most of us receive our ideas from advertisements, the media, and our schools. On the whole, it seems that we are not at ease with our freedom or using it well. How do we fit in with other people, make real connections, yet retain our individuality?

The answer must be grounded in some kind of form. Etiquette is a reference point, a place from which we can begin our inquiries. For instance, the form of a ten-day silent meditation retreat allowed me to investigate myself deeply. I was able to discover my connection to the Fall, to original sin. Shining the light of awareness on this connection has helped me to dissolve it. Gremlins such as anger, jealousy, and fear have a hard time living in the light.

## AIKIDO AS ETIQUETTE

I believe that the model of aikido offers us a light with which we can examine ourselves. Aikido has an etiquette of its own that governs all interactions and is understood in any dojo in the world. There are, of course, variations in the forms, but the meanings are always recognizable. This commonality allows people from anywhere in the world to train together even if they do not speak the same language. I have trained with people and experienced moments of intimacy, awkwardness, and humor without exchanging a single word. The form and the etiquette of aikido allow this kind of exchange to take place regardless of any difference between the participants in age, social status, race, or gender. Aikido enables us to meet, have an intense exchange, and part, communicating solely through a bodily experience. What a different way to know someone: by how they feel rather than what they say!

Aikido principles can enhance any form. Our ability to relax and to center ourselves while under pressure can be helpful in any situation. Our capacity to extend ourselves to and include others is part of what helps communities to function. We don't have to practice the formal art of aikido with its vigorous physical training: just the principles of stabilizing, opening, extending, and accepting can enhance, empower, and bring fullness and refinement to the etiquette inherent in all of our practices.

## ETIQUETTE AS A CODEPENDENT WEB

If we lack confidence in ourselves and are unable to see ourselves as intelligent, compassionate beings, then we will inevitably operate from a platform of etiquette, and our interactions will be based on agreements of social convention. Codependence, which involves a loss of self, is the generally accepted etiquette for behavior among people whose sense of morality and virtue has become obscured. We create codependent webs: we are intertwined with one another to keep alive the notion that we will support the actions of others if they support ours.

This is the etiquette of "Let's pretend." Let's pretend that if I am nice to you, then you will be nice back to me. Or, a more pathological version is, Let's pretend that if I am nice to you, then you will be mean to me. You can see all the possible combinations of pretending, from the seemingly caring to the pathological.

When the social form is emptied of morality and virtue, and interactions become hollow and meaningless, we begin to see a form of anarchy best described as pathology. Psychology has labeled many different types of pathologies, but the root of them all is an inability to make sense of or give meaning to the social etiquette by which we are all expected to abide. Pathology and all of its ramifications is one of the tragedies that can motivate us to lift ourselves to a higher level of self-fulfillment.

## THE BEGINNING OF MORALITY

With the introduction of morality, meaning begins to fill the hollow shell of etiquette. The line between etiquette and morality is not always clear. What is offered as morality is often really just social etiquette. Only if a moral principle within a person resonates as truth will it begin to guide his or her behavior. Etiquette is about practices and forms; morality is more concerned with right, wrong, and truth in relation to human character. Morality vitalizes the form of etiquette. The person concerned with self-fulfillment must go beyond the etiquette of codependent safety to a more independent, courageous vision for his or her behavior.

*chapter three*

# MORALITY

*Beneath the surface level of conditioned thinking in every one of us there is a single living spirit. The still small voice whispering to me in the depths of my consciousness is saying exactly the same thing as the voice whispering to you in your consciousness. "I want an earth that is healthy, a world at peace, and a heart filled with love."*

—Eknath Easwaran, *The Compassionate Universe*

## THE DIFFICULTY OF KNOWING WHAT IS RIGHT

I have found that it can be difficult to know what is right. There have been times when my head thought that one course of action was right and my heart felt the rightness of a different choice. Especially when it comes to emotional issues, where love and attachment are active, confusion can arise as to which course of action is correct.

As a mother, there were a number of times when I felt confused about whether and how much I should interfere in my children's lives. Their teenage years were particularly challenging. There were moments when it was not entirely clear to me whether it was time for my children to take on full responsibility for their actions and accept the repercussions, or whether I should run interference and attempt to impose restrictions that reflected my moral views. My head seemed to be the more rational voice that articulated the need for a recognition of consequences, while my heart wanted them to be happy and safe and not to have to feel the sting of consequences.

Very early in her teens, my daughter, Tiphani, matured into a great beauty. She attracted men and was drawn into the rock music scene. She was a "wild" teenager in that she went to rock concerts, dated some of the rock musicians, and either stayed out late or did not come home at all after the concerts. Finally, I reached a point where the pressure of my confusion and her behavior became so great that I realized that I could not continue the struggle with myself and with her. I didn't yet know the right thing to do. On the one hand, I felt that it was dangerous for her to be involved with the rock scene, which was rampant with drugs; on the other hand, I had been involved in the 1960s music scene myself and understood her attraction to and desire to explore that world. I knew that I could not control her, and I knew that I couldn't go on trying to change her.

It became clear to me that I needed to do what was right for me. First I had to reach deeply inside myself to recognize the rightness of what I felt to be my moral truth. Then I was able to tell her that if she continued that kind of behavior, then she could not live with me. It was one of the most difficult moments of my life. Yet it allowed me to feel and act on my own deeper truth. She ended up moving out for a number of months, but when she returned we were able to renegotiate our relationship in a way that was more workable for both of us. This led to a deepening of our relationship, which continues to grow to this day. One of the many lessons that my daughter has taught me is that I can be centered enough to say no, and still keep my heart open even though I am in pain. She has helped me learn how important it is to stop and center myself. Centering myself allows me to connect to the deep layer within that knows what is right for me. It also gives me the strength and the courage to act on that knowledge.

## CENTERING AND OPENING
## TO A DEEPER TRUTH

I find that if I can still my attention, center myself, and open my mind so that it can see the whole picture, then the right, or moral, response usually becomes apparent. Becoming still, centering, and opening is not an easy task when there is pressure from the emotions. As always, it takes an inner strength, a strength that we all can build if we are willing. If we are to truly cultivate morality, then we must find a way to infuse our relationships with the principles that foster kindness and respect for all those whom we encounter. Even as warriors, we must respect our enemies, for they show us our strengths and our weaknesses.

Aikido has given me countless opportunities to choose between my frustration and my capacity to do the right thing. I can choose to be magnanimous and not seek revenge. One of the most inspirational parts of the aikido philosophy is the intention of "giving life to all beings, and not killing or struggling with each other."[1] This moral direction comes from the founder's insight, "*Budo* is love." There are times when I can rise to this level of inspiration. Even when my partner is abusive, I can open my heart and understand that people who are abusive are in pain. There are other times, however, when I want to "get her back," to "show him what it feels like," and again I feel the struggle between my moral self, which wants to give life, and my reactive self, which seeks retribution. The training situation allows me to see these parts of myself. It informs me where I am in relation to my goal, which is the freedom of unconditional love.

As we grow in our individualism by exploring who we are and what we are capable of, there is a refining and clarifying of our moral sensibility. In some cases, an entirely new territory of ethical possibilities must be addressed. In my classes, I sometimes ask whether anyone disagrees with the statement "People who attack others do so because of their pain." No one argues with this statement, yet everyone agrees that it is very difficult to acknowledge the other person's pain while he or she is attacking you.

## THE GAP BETWEEN BELIEF AND ACTION

For most of us, there is a gap between what we believe and what we do. The Judeo-Christian commandments and the Buddhist precepts give us directions, but for many of us, it is difficult to follow rules such as not harming another or not stealing, because our sense of morality is still undeveloped. For instance, some people say that it is acceptable to harm someone else in self-defense, and finding ways to not pay taxes is considered "creative financing."

People experience a certain amount of anxiety in taking responsibility for investigating right and wrong in relation to their own actions. Without a strong center, it is difficult for people to make such a self-inquiry, for they may discover a lack of morality in themselves that is painful to see. They may want others to be perfectly honest but they may not be perfectly honest themselves. For many people, decisions about what is right and wrong are about how they feel in the moment. If they are in a bad mood and someone honks a horn or yells at them, then the other person immediately becomes their enemy. They make no moral effort to understand the circumstances of the "attack."

## CHOOSING THE GOOD

Our freedom to explore the perimeters of moral possibilities may offer us more choices than we are comfortable with. Choices mean that we can choose anything from unconditional love to retribution. What direction do we take and what is more important: the results—or how do we get those results? In *The Republic of Plato*, Plato remarks,

The soul of every man does possess the power of learning the truth and the organ to see it with; and that, just as one might have to turn the whole body round in order that the eye should see light instead of darkness, so the entire soul must be turned away from this changing world, until its eye can bear to contemplate reality and that supreme splendour which we have called the Good.[2]

When we do turn away from this "changing world," where do we turn to, where do we find this "Good" that Plato speaks of? Is there a natural magnetic pull toward basic goodness and a concern for all life? One possibility is to turn inward, to contemplate the questions, Who am I? and Why do I exist? A moment of contemplation can help us find the positive direction for our ethical compass.

I have also found it helpful to look to nature for meaning. Mother Nature has taught me many lessons about patience, generosity, and expansiveness. I have seen that after a fire has burned a forest, in only one or two years, the generosity of new growth revitalizes the area. Standing at the edge of the ocean, I can feel its expansiveness in my body. The redwoods, tall and stately, hundreds of years old, are the embodiment of elegance and patience. Going to nature helps me to remember these truths and encourages me to do my part to support this goodness.

## DISCIPLINE LEADS TO FULFILLMENT

Training the center—a calm, stable place within ourselves—and the discipline of practicing returning to the center, naturally encourages more ethical behavior. When we practice, we can experiment. We can explore what happens if we are more stable and relaxed.

In my own experience, my centering practice helps me to behave more ethically and morally. I remind myself that this is a continuous process, that I must keep practicing the form. If I stop the practice, then my ability to choose the good begins to diminish. Just as cardiovascular health is maintained by regular workouts, so ethical and moral health can be maintained by regular training. A friend who was doing research work with the military told me that he discovered that the men who studied a martial art tended to be less violent at home and out in the civilian world than those who studied hand-to-hand combat.

There is a saying in the military: "Under duress, we don't rise to our expectations: we fall to our level of training." We can have insights, ideals, or brilliant ideas, but they won't necessarily manifest as our experience when we are stressed. It takes discipline, strength, and endurance to bring these insights, ideals, and ideas to life. When they do come to life, we feel exhilaration and fulfillment, as if we have somehow tapped into the natural order of things. Self-cultivation— working with form and discipline—gives us the capability of manifesting our inner morality for longer and longer periods of time.

## RIGHT LIVELIHOOD

There is a spiritual viewpoint that the form of a practice may contain within it an organic movement that cultivates considerate, humanitarian behavior. Buddhism, for example, has the concept of Right Livelihood, which is a commitment to not cause harm in the course of earning a living. However, in our society, there is a strong emphasis on the importance of getting the job done: we get paid to accomplish a task.

So what happens when getting the job done means that someone else suffers? For example, suppose that one person is required to fire another person or that one person loses custody of a child or possession of property. Is morality on the side of accomplishing the task or on the side of not inflicting suffering on another? This is not an easy question to answer, but through awareness, it may be possible to minimize the suffering that we cause another. By paying close attention to our actions, it is possible to recognize that which will cause harm and, at times, choose not to speak or act in such a way. We can at least work with our intent to decrease our personal animosity. Sometimes simple acts of consideration can have a profound effect. For instance, we could encourage ourselves to be more kind and compassionate toward other drivers when we are on the road. Considering how much most of us drive, an intention to be compassionate could make quite a difference!

## PAYING ATTENTION TO OUR THOUGHTS

Thoughts, although they can't be seen, have a feeling of substance, of weight. It has been said that thoughts are things. Some thoughts "weigh us down." We know how powerful the feelings of anxiety, depression, and anger are. Often we don't take the time to examine them carefully: we don't inquire into their origin. Instead, we move further from the origin, and, energetically, further from our center.

If we take the time to do the practice of mindfulness, then we can cultivate the act of paying attention to our thoughts. If we see that we have recurring negative thoughts, such as judgment or resentment, then the desire to be free from such thoughts may arise. This will encourage positive, ethical behavior, because each human being has, in his or her essence of being, a tendency toward basic goodness.

The practice of looking deeply into ourselves is similar to our Western scientific investigation into the origin of matter and the universe. I may ask the same type of questions that scientists ask: Is there a tendency toward ethical order in my life? Does my basic structure have encoded in it an intrinsically harmonious connection to the universe?

## SAINTS AND MYSTICS AS HINTS

An individual's journey toward discovering his or her ethical and moral essence is a personal one. An individual can read the experiences of the great saints and mystics. Their stories may touch the person, and he or she may feel a resonance with their experiences. Ultimately, however, they are still *their* experiences. Each person must make his or her own way toward the source of life. The best that a teacher or teaching can do is drop a hint. The person must take the hint, for if he or she is to behave in a mature and kind way, then the urge must come from deep within.

Rising from the chaos of anarchy, etiquette is the form that allows an investigation of morality to take place. When we move outside the form, we begin to lose the stability of the form. In aikido and Conscious Embodiment work, we cultivate a specific, embodied form that represents a centered, stable experience. Within that form, there is a calm, still point, which we call center. When we work with this form, we experience movements or shifts of attention that cause instability. A certain amount of instability is dynamic, but a great deal of instability arouses too much energy, triggering feelings of anxiety or fear, which tend to lead to unethical or inappropriate behavior.

The question is, If we are faithful to our centering discipline, if we cultivate increased awareness in our lives, will we naturally begin to behave in an ethical, moral way? The experiment is for each of us to make. Only by making the experiment will we find out the truth for ourselves.

## OUR MORAL COMPASS

As my practice has deepened through the years, I have begun to respect the feeling or line of my moral compass. A compass has a needle that points, or makes a line to, due north, and a person uses this needle to find his or her way. Through the years, I have become less confused about knowing when I am on the right track. When I can bring myself to a calm, still place, my moral compass can show me the way, the line of my direction.

I believe that everybody has access to this kind of inner guidance.

It must be cultivated and respected if it is to become a valid part of our decision-making process. Respect also means that we understand our limitations and boundaries in terms of how close we are to or how far we stray from that directional line. Sometimes we get information from our feelings: feelings of uneasiness and feelings of clarity can give us hints.

## RESPECT

If we are to genuinely respect others, then we must first respect ourselves. To do this, we need to be able to see ourselves as part of an amazing creation. The human species is a remarkable step in the evolution of life. It is easy to overlook human life and be drawn into the frustrations and difficulties that we encounter. I find it helpful to remember that I am connected to something larger than myself. It is difficult to articulate, but I will call that something the divine. When I consider that I am connected to the divine, which is found in heaven and on Earth alike, I experience respect for myself. It is a question of remembering to see myself in this way. I can make the choice to relate to the challenges of life with appreciation and respect. Choosing such a view of life means that I feel more energetic, more alive.

In India, holy men and women often begin and end their interactions with the word *namaste*. It is sometimes translated as "I respect the light within you." In the aikido dojo, the student bows toward others and the training space. The respectful word and the respectful gesture: each is a statement of appreciation.

With continued practice, there can be an added feeling within the form that springs from personal experience. Respect and appreciation engender care and consideration. As the relationship develops, a person's feelings of respect can increase if his or her behavior resonates with his or her mind, heart, and soul. Respect is then a willing response rising out of appreciation. A feeling of respect for another is an internal gauge of a person's sense of moral rightness in the relationship.

This sense of moral rightness is what gives the green light to inner feelings of trust and openness, which can occur when there is a moral resonance between one person and the actions of another person.

It is possible for us to think too much and do too little: to intellectualize and not practice the techniques or movements that allow us to observe, develop, and strengthen ourselves under pressure. In order to discover and understand the roots of our thoughts, to observe how we function morally, we must actually do the practice. Self-respect and an appreciation of the practice give us the energy to continue. The principles we cultivate, such as centering or being relaxed and open under pressure, are the same whether we practice aikido, Conscious Embodiment, meditation, yoga, or any other discipline. These principles emerge from a sense of moral rightness. It is from this sense of moral rightness that we can cultivate our capacity to become stable, relaxed, and compassionate. Perhaps this is the place where Plato's "Good" comes from.

The mind and the body need to be in balance. I believe that this balance should be a dynamic: a being and doing between thought and action. This means that the practitioner has to take responsibility for his or her own schedule and practice time. It may mean that the practitioner works with the guidance of an experienced teacher.

In the Eastern disciplines, where there is a strong tradition of surrendering to the teacher, moral guidance often comes from the teacher. In fact, in many cases, students are required to obey the teacher. In the West, we tend to be suspicious of authority. The result is that we do what we feel like in the moment, thus losing the clarity of discipline and the direction of our line, our moral compass. Our energy becomes diluted and our self-respect begins to dwindle.

Perhaps by integrating the Eastern and Western perspectives, we can find a dynamic balance. If so, we may be able to move more fluidly and freely between these two methods of self-development. Discipline and flexibility are two sides of self-cultivation and the development of mature moral standards. Our commitment to our path and practice is a statement of self-respect. Self-respect can open the door to relaxation and confidence.

## EXPLORING OUR FEAR

In *The American Heritage Dictionary* (second college edition), *fear* is defined as "an emotion of alarm and agitation caused by the expectation or realization of danger."[3] Regarding the economic tumult of the 1930s, Franklin D. Roosevelt said, "The only thing we have to fear is fear itself." Fear, in an abstract sense, is an amount of energy that triggers a subjective response that involves physiological changes. If we can step back and observe these changes, then we can relate to fear from a reasonable or logical point of view.

But our physiology often doesn't allow us to be objective. When we are afraid, we are right in the middle of the fear. We are reacting to, rather than interested in, the situation. Our sense of humor is absent. The stimulation of the sympathetic nervous system triggers the fight or flight response. Flexibility and options are intrinsic to freedom. Therefore, when we lose our flexibility and our options, we lose our freedom.

Fear is triggered by loss of control. When we or the things around us get out of control, fear and insecurity arise. Once again, a dread of chaos and a fear of descending to emotional anarchy begin to lurk beneath the surface. When we try to keep control, we often tense up and contract. So how do we deal with our fear in a way that it will not undermine our morality?

In aikido practice, our partner can represent fear. At times, I experience genuine fear when my partner is powerful and the attacks are fast and strong. When I am afraid, it is difficult to perform techniques in a way that is open and nonresistant. Throughout the years, practice on the mat has allowed me to get to know my fear.

In my day-to-day life, I tend to find ways to distract myself: planning, judging, and carrying out activities keep me from feeling my fear. On the mat, it is more difficult to distract myself. The only other possibilities are to resist or to collapse: the whole thing is raw and exposed. I have found that if I can expose the fear, accept it, and ground it, my system learns to tolerate the energy, and eventually a recycling process occurs in which the energy of the fear is used positively in the interaction.

From the aikido standpoint, the best way to deal with an attack—and I think that it is fair to call fear an attack—is to center and open to or face the situation, which in this case is the fear itself. If we have a form or etiquette and an understanding of the principles of right and wrong, then it is possible to have enough stability to face and investigate the fear. In a meditation situation, the mindfulness approach encourages us to stop, settle down, and look at our fear.

The next step is to ask what drives this fear and where it comes from. As soon as we are able to ask these questions, we are less caught up in the fear experience. We have stepped outside of the panic enough to wonder. This wondering opens things up a little.

Most fear is the result of memory. We may begin to see how the fear is directly connected with a memory and that the memory is, by definition, from the past, not the present. If we disengage from the past by bringing our attention to the present moment, then we may experience a diminishing of the fear. Fear, like all incoming forces, uses resistance to gather energy and increase power. Nonresistance—looking and accepting—begin to diminish the force of the incoming fear.

## ORDEALS: TESTING THE PERIMETERS
## OF OUR DEVELOPMENT

Franz E. Winkler articulates the difficulties inherent in personal growth: "The goal sought since time immemorial is the finding of the Self, but the way toward that goal is steep and thorny, for it is also the strenuous way to freedom, to peace, and to happiness."[4]

Facing our fear is an ordeal, and the ordeal can be an opportunity. Going through ordeals historically has been a way to develop strength and the freedom to function in areas that had previously felt too threatening. This leads us to the questions, What will be the result of our ordeal? Will it be positive or negative? Will it awaken a surrender to a deeper layer of our morality—to greater goodness, integrity, and compassion—or will it trigger a lust for power? If the outcome of the ordeal is successful, then our sense of moral rightness is increased. There is a new or added confidence in our sense of our place in the world. A rite of passage can open a door to a more expansive and confident state of being. It can also open the door to more possibilities and responsibilities. This new state—less constrictive, more expansive—can feel frightening as well as empowering.

There are also ordeals, such as natural disasters or life-threatening illnesses, that arise more spontaneously. In these cases, we don't involve ourselves willingly in the situation. We suddenly find ourselves in the middle of a frightening and painful situation. Sometimes this kind of experience can be totally overwhelming, and instead of expanding to meet the situation, we may contract and become paralyzed and traumatized by the event. Instead of dissolving a layer of fear, this type of situation increases the fear. As fear increases, we lose mobility, confidence, and a sense of freedom. Instead, we feel trapped.

George Leonard, my dear friend and longtime partner at Aikido of Tamalpais, in Mill Valley, California, maintains that aikido offers a wonderful opportunity in the form of the black belt test. He says that there are few opportunities in adult life to consciously choose to undergo an ordeal, which is what training for and taking a black belt test is. This ordeal—this rite of passage—could be seen as an exercise that increases feelings of self-worth. This right of passage allows us an opportunity to grow, to expand beyond our present limitations, which increases our feelings of competence and confidence and our ability to lead moral lives.

Although a black belt test, or a vision quest, or even a military exercise is unlikely to have life-or-death consequences, participants have a sense of all or nothing, a sense that they are putting themselves on the line: either all will be lost or a leap will be made. This leap is into a greater realm of existence, and something happens as a result of this leap. An ordeal, such as a black belt test, a vision quest, or a military exercise, can be a challenging and exciting event when we face it willingly. In this case, there is some foreknowledge, some sense that the upcoming event will have moments that will be difficult, even frightening, or painful. Nonetheless, participants willingly submit to the situation, encouraged by the possibility of growth.

Accepting the assignment implies that we are looking for something that will add knowledge and confidence to our lives. Usually, we have some anxiety that we won't do well, or maybe fail completely. But by going through the process, we face this fear and become stronger. When we look back on the ordeal, we realize that we were able to survive and function and that we have expanded our sense of ourselves. We have less of a sense of limitation. We are less stuck, freer to move forward in our self-development.

## READJUSTING TO INCREASED ABILITIES

As a student opens up to a more powerful experience of himself or herself, he or she becomes disconnected from former relationships and the social etiquette that had previously defined his or her life. The student is alone, separate from the familiar codependent web. This can be a challenging moment. He or she may wish to renounce this newfound freedom and individuality and return to the old, familiar identity of the smaller, more limited self.

This is where commitment, training, and practice will help him or her to adjust to a new identity, which, on the one hand, implies more expansiveness and freedom, and, on the other hand, more responsibility. The student can no longer relate to his or her friends and situation in the same way. The game has changed. The student may, for a time, feel a freedom from the pressures and old limitations: he or she can do more now. However, the question of what to do with his or her new abilities creates a new pressure: the larger pressure of responsibility.

## RESPONSIBILITY

Like most of us, I was indoctrinated with the idea that I must learn to be responsible for my behavior and my possessions. As a child, I resisted this pressure to behave politely and treat my possessions gently. There were exceptions to my stance, however, and they were my relationships with my invalid mother and horses. In those relationships, I tried to meet the challenge of being present and doing my part, even when I was unhappy or uncomfortable. I think that I was able to extend myself in these areas because I felt an innate connection with my mother and with horses, and I saw an intrinsic value in these relationships.

Becoming a mother was another intense awakening into another level of responsibility. The pressure to handle this added level of responsibility came from deep within me. I experienced it on three levels: instinctive, intuitive, and cognitive. The instinctive level of responsibility is easily seen in wild animals. It was amazing to feel how deep and primitive those feelings were in me. Sometimes I experienced difficult moments of conflict between my cognitive and my instinctive levels of responsibility. I remember an occasion when a relative wanted to hold my newborn. The cognitive part of me saw this as a good thing that would reaffirm family connections. The instinctive part of me did not want this person to touch my baby. I allowed my baby to be held, feeling uncomfortable about it, while reminding myself that this was good for family relations. My intuition was the tiebreaker in this case: I understood that no harm would come from this interaction.

*Responsibility* has its roots in *respondēre,* a Latin word that means "to respond."[5] *The American Heritage Dictionary* (second college edition) defines *responsible* as "implies trustworthy performance of fixed duties and consequent awareness of the penalty for failure to do them."[6] "Fixed duties" are about form, about things being a particular way, and about the intention to maintain that particular way in order to keep other's confidence.

## RESPONSIBILITY TO SELF

The process of accepting more responsibility starts by being present to ourselves. Conscious Embodiment is one way that a person can cultivate a relationship with his or her self. This is done by achieving a state called dropped attention, in which the student brings his or her focus back to his or her self, body, and energy. The student uses centering techniques to recall attention to the present moment in order to review the basic alignment of mind and body. He or she rotates attention around four focus points: the breath, the balance of the surrounding energy field or presence, the sensation of gravity, and a quality, which is a word representing a positive aspect of consciousness. Qualities often used include *acceptance, compassion, patience, softness,* and *appreciation.* By evoking the quality now and then throughout the day, the feeling begins to become a genuine part of the student's identity.

Being present with ourselves in the moment is a basic function of mindfulness. This kind of internal focus is seen in the Buddhist style of *shamatha* (peacefulness) meditation, which is the practice of seeing with precision the situation at every moment. In aikido, we cultivate the ability to maintain a strong center when we are attacked, so that we can see and sense with great precision the speed, power, and form of the attack. Instead of tensing up, we can use our stability to relax, open, get information, and respond appropriately.

## RESPONSIBILITY TO OTHERS

Once we are able to work with ourselves honestly, we have the next level of responsibility to work with, which is the responsibility of dealing with other people. In the terminology of Conscious Embodiment, *open attention* is the state that addresses our relationship with others. When we practice open attention, we expand our field of awareness to make room for and include others. We welcome them into our territory and willingly stabilize the space for them. In this model, we are not responsible for the people themselves: rather, we take responsibility for the environment that they have entered.

This is an important distinction. In this way of working, we accept others as they are: we do not try to change them. Instead, we provide them with a stable, calm environment and unconditional acceptance. We set an example for them by cultivating an environment of calmness and kindness, thus silently articulating the positive aspect of morality. Similarly, in aikido, we welcome the attacker into our territory: we blend with and include his or her energy, changing the entire situation in a positive way.

Being responsible for someone or something means that we willingly increase the size of our territory. We set aside any personal agenda and work in a larger context so that whomever or whatever we are including will have a supportive environment in which to function. We go beyond ourselves and our small world without relinquishing our own centeredness. This is a leap into the next level. We no longer look out for ourselves alone. Our moral compass extends beyond the boundaries of right and wrong: we have entered the territory of compassion.

*chapter four*

# COMPASSION

*The ability to see all existence from a non-self-centered perspective
is central to the Shintō identity with nature and also constitutes what
Buddhism calls wisdom, which in its highest expression is none other
than compassion.*

—Taitetsu Unno, foreword to Kisshomaru Ueshiba, *Spirit of Aikido*

## NURTURING THE SEED OF COMPASSION

Many times I have found myself standing in front of my training
partner and experiencing intense fear. Sometimes it was the look in
my partner's eyes that would trigger the fear. I know why O'Sensei
says, "Don't look at the opponent's eyes, or your mind will be drawn
into his eyes."[1] I would try to look away, shift my attention back into
my body, and tell myself, *Feel your feet, legs, and hips. Open yourself.
Let this person in, include him.* These are the moments in training
where I know that I can grow, the moments that stretch me by asking me to go beyond my feelings of fear, inadequacy, and anger and
choose compassion instead. Facing a partner whom I know to be
strong and powerful while I feel fearful and inadequate, I can choose
compassion instead of anger. Typically, I deal with my fear by becoming frustrated. I tend to respond by trying to get my opponent before
he gets me. The alternative that aikido philosophy offers is that of
openness and nonresistance. It is through training and practice that

these seeds of compassion are nurtured and can grow within me.

I am continually amazed by the ability of my teacher, Saotome Sensei, to sustain his open, beautiful posture while under attack from large, strong men. It is inspiring to see how easily he flows through situations where there are multiple attackers. He is often smiling, his shoulders are relaxed, and he is moving, yet he is still at his center. He exemplifies how a strong foundation and an open heart can transform the hardness of aggression into the softness of connection. He embodies compassion, openness, and warmth in the face of aggression.

## CULTIVATING OPENNESS UNDER PRESSURE

Cultivating openness under pressure is one of the great gifts of aikido practice. To expand and keep the heart open in this type of situation is *not* an easy task. But with O'Sensei's vision and Saotome Sensei's embodied example, I have been encouraged to move forward along the path. It is easy to lose sight of love and acceptance as the intensity of practice escalates. Again and again, I have to remember the importance of the teaching *"Budo* is love."

Some years ago the Dalai Lama gave a talk on compassion. He said that maybe the word *compassion* was not practical enough: perhaps, he suggested, words such as *warmth* and *affection* were more closely related to the feeling that he was trying to convey. I think that he realized that for most people in the Western world, compassion is a "good idea," but not a practical way to advance in a competitive culture. Perhaps he thought that if he could make the concept of compassion sound less exalted and more accessible, more ordinary, then more people would practice it.

## KINDNESS

I find it helpful to remember that kindness needs to start in the most ordinary places of my life. It needs to start in my own home, within myself. There was a period in my life when I was deeply unhappy. My marriage was on the rocks, and I was ashamed of my lack of patience as a mother. Ironically, it was a time when, to the outside world, my life looked fine and successful: I should have been happy. Then a friend who was teaching *vipassana*, a type of mindfulness meditation, invited one of his teachers from India to teach at a retreat in our area. Knowing my background in meditation, he suggested that I have an interview with her. I entered the room where she was seated and began to settle myself on the cushion in front of her. Before I could even settle into a position of stillness, she turned to the interpreter and said something in Hindi. He said to me, "She says don't even bother to do *vipassana* right now; do only *metta* (loving kindness)."

I was startled. Usually the student asks a question and the teacher responds. "Why?" I asked. Again, she said something in Hindi, and the interpreter translated: "Your 'this life' is in trouble, and you need to work on it now, so do only *metta*." He then motioned that the interview was at an end.

I was stunned. The entire interaction had taken probably two minutes. I knew that the term "this life" meant my feelings toward myself. Clearly, she had seen my unhappiness, and the antidote she had prescribed was loving kindness.

The loving kindness practice she was referring to starts with the self. Typically, the person repeats the phrase, *May I be happy, may I be peaceful, may I be filled with love.* The benediction then expands out, first to loved ones, and then to all beings, and then returns to the self. I was shocked to find that, at first, I could not bring myself to wish for happiness, peace, and love myself. My self-loathing was too great. I found that I could use thoughts about my children to awaken feelings of love. Then for a brief time I could wish these same feelings for myself, but it was difficult.

I began to see that trying to be nice to others while disliking myself was painful and exhausting. I persevered with the practice, reciting the form inwardly many times a day. At first, I couldn't feel a positive response, but I continued to recite the words. It took about three months before I could begin to feel some genuine warmth toward myself. At the end of six months, I could feel a definite shift in myself when I would bring my attention to the practice. I could feel more softness, openness, and even affection. I still had bouts of self-hatred from time to time, but there were wonderful moments of respite in which I could feel some genuine warmth and kindness toward myself.

## BUILDING A RESERVOIR OF POSITIVE FEELINGS

An attitude of gentleness or a gesture of tenderness toward ourselves affects how we experience the world. Words are a way of calling the attention to an area. They can only begin to convey the richness and fullness of compassion's territory, but they are a beginning and they can be helpful. We need to find how to transform words and ideas into sensations and felt experiences. I would say to myself, *May I be happy so that I can spread happiness.* Then I would visualize a golden light surrounding me and spreading out to include my family and friends. I would try to imagine a warm sensation, such as the pleasant feeling of sunlight on my body. In time, as these practices became more tangible, more real, the experience became stronger. Building a reservoir of positive inner feelings gives us strength, so that we can address the more shadowy parts of ourselves. Ultimately, it is these shadowy parts that we need to hold and accept in the warm heart of our compassion. Until we can truly open and accept ourselves—all of ourselves—we will not be free.

Compassion ("the deep feeling of sharing the suffering of another, together with the inclination to give aid or support," according to *The American Heritage Dictionary* [second college edition][2]) opens the door to interconnection. This is the point of view from which we see that we are intrinsically connected to all of the universe. We go beyond etiquette, which dictates that some things are "none of our business." And we go beyond the moral boundaries of right and wrong, which say that someone deserves to suffer because his or her actions do not fit into our moral view. We open to the willingness to acknowledge and relate to the suffering or joy of another. This becomes possible because our centering practice reveals a positive inner core. This core gives us the strength to be sensitive to and considerate of others.

As we begin to expand and include others, we respond to the sense of connectedness that is implicit in the universe. In my daily meditation I sometimes contemplate the question, *Who am I?* Whatever arises as a response, I ask myself, *Where does this come from?* The end result of this questioning process is that I often experience myself as a pattern of vibrating atoms and molecules. Because everything in the universe is made up of vibrating atoms and molecules, I feel connected to all things.

My understanding of my own interconnectedness with all things encourages me to open myself. During my time working in prison, I heard some heart-wrenching stories. Some of the women felt that while they were in prison their children were being abused by other family members. Their inability to protect them was a source of incredible pain. As difficult as it was, I tried to be there with them. I could help by acknowledging the pain, and grounding it in compassion. I would speak the same words of my loving kindness practice and use the same visualization: "May they be happy and surrounded by golden light." As we expand and open our hearts, we willingly tolerate more and more feelings and intensity of emotion.

How can we do this without feeling overburdened? Hazrat Inayat Khan says it beautifully: "The bringers of joy have always been the children of sorrow."[3] The ability to love is directly related to the ability to tolerate pain. When we open ourselves to the pain, the whole situation becomes more spacious. The space around us has a buoyancy and it nurtures us, just as it nurtures all things in the universe. The more we open ourselves and relate to the whole of life, the more its elements of joy and sorrow, of space and energy, can become a supporting part of our process of unfoldment.

When I was young I never would have made the association between responsibility and resilience. I remember feeling responsible for my mother because I wasn't able to heal her or at least help her more. I felt helpless and guilty. I struggled with my feelings of responsibility. It was my resistance to the situation that made it so painful and problematic for me. Since that time I have found that when I accept a situation fully, I experience less suffering and the responsibility is easy to carry.

## EXTENDING OURSELVES TO OTHERS

Sometimes responsibility can show up suddenly in a person's life, such as when a family member or friend becomes ill. Or a person may be required by inheritance to become responsible for something. In either case, something more is being asked of a person than simply looking out for himself or herself. At these moments the individual holds the possibility of opening: widening the spirit to include what has been placed before him or her. Aikido gives a person the way to practice this widening: it helps to build the strength that a person needs to willingly extend himself or herself to others.

*Mahayana* (the greater vehicle) practices, which are part of the Buddhist tradition, are based on helping others. *Mahayana* facilitates the liberation of all sentient beings: everyone and everything is included in this vision. This is O'Sensei's vision as well. He says, "A mind to serve for the peace of all human beings in the world is needed in Aikido."[4]

All of this requires a sense of expansion. I have found that without a firm foundation, expansion will only jeopardize the whole situation. Stability is demonstrated by the confidence that we can maintain calm presence, and flexibility shows that we can stay open and so facilitate change. A strong foundation provides us with the confidence that we need in order to relax, be calm, and, if it is appropriate, provide direction. It is easy to wish to stay open and loving under pressure. But it is only through practice that we actually can develop the strength to stay open and present, widening ourselves while sustaining our connection with and concern for others.

## THE QUALITIES OF COMPASSION

Compassion has many qualities. Traditionally, these qualities are described through images of earth, sky, fire, and water. There is the embracing quality of the earth. There is the heat of the fire, which burns up our resistance. There is the soft fluidity of water or the delicate moisture of the morning dew sparkling on the flowers and grasses that bring life and nourishment and quench the thirsty soul. Just as plants tend to expand in moisture and contract in dryness, so our hearts tend to open in the presence of compassion and close in the presence of criticism. The ability to have an open heart is present in all of us. Just as our bodies hold a great capacity for strength, so our hearts have a great capacity for love. By conditioning our bodies, we bring out the strength; by opening our hearts, we bring out the love. It is possible to develop, little by little, a heart that can stay open under pressure.

As we speed around attending to the tasks of our day, it is easy to forget to open our hearts and have genuine concern for all with whom we come in contact. We want to get things done rather than communicate with who or what is before us. Through the cultivation of compassion, the open heart teaches us to accept the whole situation of life as it is: the light and the shadow, the good and the bad. Compassion does not reject: it accepts. This acceptance is part of the alchemical or transformative process that can change hardness into softness, and change sorrow into joy.

## COMPASSIONATE LEADERSHIP

As responsibility and compassion grow within us, they naturally expand outward into leadership. Leadership in its positive sense willingly generates energy in a way that is caring and inspirational. A good leader tends to be positive, confident, and considerate in situations. Ideally, this confidence has a magnetic quality that inspires, rather than forces, people to participate in the task at hand. Our capacity for sustaining compassion under pressure can be a model, an inspiration, for others.

Nelson Mandela is a wonderful example of such a leader. Twenty-seven years of imprisonment never deterred his commitment to his vision of freedom: freedom not only for the black people of South Africa, but for all people. I was in South Africa in 1997. While there, I visited the prison on Robben Island where Nelson Mandela was jailed. It is now a museum, and the tour guides are men who were imprisoned with Nelson Mandela. Our guide told us that when he first arrived on the island, he wanted revenge for the treatment that he had received. Mandela told him that to seek revenge would put him at the same level as his jailers. "We must show them," he said, "the way that we would like to be treated by treating them with the same respect and fairness that we would want."[5]

To have a vision and to accomplish a task, energy is needed. The energy can come from resistance or from inspiration. Leadership that derives its energy from the open, compassionate heart has the potential to heal our society and bring balance back to our lives. This kind of leadership will be followed willingly, for it is supportive, not demanding.

## RESPONSIBILITY AND AMBITION

Ambition is of particular interest to me, because I have had ambivalent feelings about ambition since childhood. I have always admired those who have a clear sense of what they want and proceed unhesitatingly along the path to their goal. But I have always inwardly criticized those who achieve their goal at the expense of others. Perhaps because I was not clear as to exactly what it was that I wanted, I could never get clear as to how to proceed. I think that my lack of clarity was because I was afraid that the shadowy, greedy parts of myself would get out of control, and, like those I so criticized, my achievements would be at someone else's expense.

I have come to see ambition as a positive part of the process of traveling the road to happiness and freedom. A strong desire that is fueled by ambition seems to be a necessary ingredient in the creative process. The fundamental question is, What is the source of this ambition? Ambition can arise from a place of inspiration and abundance, or from a place of impoverishment and insecurity. When ambition arises from abundance, the quality of leadership tends to be colored by the gentle and positive characteristics of compassion, and a great deal can be accomplished in a "win–win" fashion.

Ambition that has compassion as its foundation communicates *We are in this thing together,* rather than *Me first!* Compassionate ambition has an underlying theme of abundance: there is enough for everybody, and we want to make sure that everybody has enough. We make the effort to support others. Ambition that has impoverishment as its foundation willingly sacrifices the individual to the goal. It is based on the notion of separation rather than unity.

The aikido mat is a lens that can help us to look more carefully at this issue. Each aikido technique is an event that has a beginning, a middle, and an end. The aikido student wants to be successful, that is, to throw or pin his or her partner. If, however, that is the student's sole ambition, then he or she will experience a particular feeling of force or aggression in the movement. If, on the other hand, the student's ambition is to achieve a feeling of unification and, through that, complete the technique, then he or she will experience a feeling that is more akin to dancing, and the technique will be executed through nonresistance.

When I am the person being thrown, it feels unpleasant when I am secondary to the outcome. Not only is it unpleasant, it triggers an urge in me to resist. When my partner's ambition is more focused on making a connection with me as a partner, I not only find the throw more satisfying, I am much less inclined to resist. The result is that the throw is accomplished, and I come away from the encounter feeling nurtured, not dominated.

People prefer to live in a supportive way, rather than with an underlying sense of impoverishment. But how can we find the confidence to act from a place of generosity rather than avarice? How do we make generosity and compassion the root of our personal survival? How do we move in an organic way from the etiquette of social survival to a moral direction, and, beyond that, to a genuine warmth toward and affection for others while we are in a leadership role?

## MINDFULNESS

One classic technique is to investigate the nature of this "self" that manifests ambition or compassion. In this mode of self-inquiry, the practitioner becomes quiet and begins to observe the thoughts and feelings that arise in the mind. This type of self-cultivation is sometimes called mindfulness. By stopping, sitting silently, and observing his or her mental state, the practitioner can begin to discover the inner workings of the mind, finding the roots of altruism and the roots of dominance. What the practitioner may discover is that underneath the posturing, defensiveness, and neediness lies a calm, open, awakened state that does not have to struggle to maintain an identity or a connection.

For this type of practice, we need discipline in order to be still, not just in our bodies but in our attention. By becoming still, even for a few seconds, we can observe the inception of a thought. We can watch it form, and if we don't attach any emotion to it, then we will see it dissolve. We can then ask ourselves, *Where does this thought come from? From memory? From intuition? From the collective unconscious?*

By observing our thoughts, we begin to see what motivates us. Ambition itself is not the issue. What is important is how we respond to the energy of desire within the ambition. Our ability for leadership is defined by how well we manage this energy. If we have done our homework and looked deeply at our motivation, then we will be better able to handle the energy skillfully. Leadership is best exemplified and most satisfying when the leader's motivation arises from a desire to serve rather than to gratify the self. In this context, the leader's service will constitute a positive outcome for all. If our ambition is based on a wish to serve, then our leadership will be supportive and compassionate.

## REPETITION OF PRACTICE

When I was young, one of my favorite books was *The Black Stallion*. In this story, there was a bond of love between a horse and a boy that was so deep that the horse would respond to the boy without hesitation. In the book, the bond of love developed in a day or two. In real life, I discovered, this process takes longer. True, you can begin the process in a day or two, and definite progress can be made. But time and an attitude of commitment are required in order for the relationship to mature.

I once was given a horse for almost no money because she was mean and ornery, and no one wanted to deal with her. After almost a year, I could jump her through a course without a bridle or saddle. She had become my closest companion. I worked with her every day and occasionally slept in her stall. It was through the repetition of practice that we were able to achieve this relationship.

## RELATIONSHIP WITH OURSELVES

One of the first steps that we take in our journey toward happiness and freedom is to develop a relationship with ourselves. In order to learn more about ourselves, we need to pause, to take a break from our external activities, and to begin the process of self-examination. Becoming still and using inquiry allows the intuition to offer its wisdom. Intuition comes from within. We can develop a positive relationship with ourselves by learning how to gain access to our own inner wisdom. In time, through our practice, we can discover the repressed parts of ourselves. Accepting these parts can help us to feel strong and confident.

I have found that as I examine the roots of feelings such as abandonment, if I become still for a moment and use my intuition, instead of an absence, there is a presence, a sense of connection. It does not show up in the way that I originally expected, the fairy tale version, but it shows up in a place deep in my psyche that informs me that, subatomically, everything is connected. As Newton points out, for every action there is an equal and opposite reaction. Everything we do affects everything else.

From time to time I have wondered what it is that creates the coherence that we find in the world of particles. In his book *The Universe Is a Green Dragon: A Cosmic Creation Story,* Brian Schwimm suggests that the cohering principle be called love.[6] Whatever we call it, my own awareness that interconnection exists has created a sense of responsibility in me, a responsibility that is supported by an ethical intention. At its most basic level, it manifests itself as the urge to not make things worse. At its best, it wishes to bring life and love to all things. When I am paying attention, it produces a feeling of respect, kindness, and compassion for life and all things that make up existence.

When I took on the challenge of working with the horse that no one wanted, I knew that I could make an instant connection with her. What I wanted to explore was whether that connection could be a deep and lasting one. Only time would tell, for relationships are mysterious. What is not mysterious is the fact that cultivating compassion in a relationship makes it stronger.

I am grateful for my practice in aikido and meditation. Both forms have allowed me to use inquiry as a light that has shown me parts of myself that needed to be recognized and accepted before they could be released. With continued practice, my inquiry has shed light on some of the shadowy, ugly places inside of me. As my compassion has grown, so has my ability to hold those places. It is clear that when I can accept those parts of myself, I am less critical of others. When I am not so busy judging and comparing, I feel more free. This ongoing process is nurtured in the light of the practice of inquiry. The more that compassion is practiced, the stronger it grows.

## FORM AND IMPROVISATION

When I was a young girl, my obsession with horses was respected and supported with riding lessons. I began training—that is, learning to ride correctly—when I was five. Until that time, I had ridden ponies at my friends' houses. We always played and had fun on the ponies. Sometimes when a pony bolted I got scared, but mostly I had fun. It was a good introduction to horses, because it was casual and based on feeling without form.

Then I began to take riding lessons on horses, and the focus shifted. Everything became more serious. Now there was more emphasis on form and repetition. At that time, I loved the form. I loved to see horses and riders focused and working together, creating elegant, flowing lines as they jumped over hurdles and moved in prescribed circular movements around the ring. I knew that in order to be able to do that, I needed to practice again and again until smoothness and confidence moved through me into the horse, and we brought the form to elegant, fluid life.

For the next three or four years, I concentrated completely on form. Then, when I was about nine, I started wanting to ride out on the trails again. I wanted to ride bareback, lie on my horse while she grazed, or wander down tree-covered lanes in the fall, watching the brilliantly colored leaves floating gently to the ground. I was drawn to the formless, the intuitive, the pure sensation side of riding. I still trained, but some days, and often after practice, I would go out, away from the ring, and let whatever happened happen.

I think that I was finding the balance between form and improvisation. Of course, in the classical sense, there is freedom and improvisation within the form, but it is a different thing altogether to allow the situation to create itself spontaneously, without any mental intention clarifying the direction. But there has to be a reference point, a basic level of skill, something that allows freedom and spontaneity without the situation becoming chaotic or without the practitioner feeling lost.

The reference point, or skill level, is cultivated through practice. It was the years of training that gave me enough confidence in myself and my horse that I knew that I could afford to let things unfold. I was not afraid that I would get lost or have problems with my horse. I was confident that we could go out and explore, and be able to make it home before dark. The result was that I could relax and enjoy our adventure. I found that I still wanted to and did continue practicing, and I was able at appropriate times to relax the form and allow things to unfold. I never felt any fear on these occasions, although sometimes the adults would imply that I should. What I felt instead was my open heart, and my deep love for my horse and the beauty of nature.

## THE PRESENT IS AN ACQUIRED TASTE

One of my teachers, Tibetan Buddhist Chögyam Trungpa Rinpoche, says, "Compassion contains fundamental fearlessness, fearlessness without hesitation."[7] My experience of fearlessness comes when I am less focused on what might happen and more aware of what is happening. The more I focus on what is happening and the more I practice openness, the less afraid I feel. Mindfulness, attention to the present moment, and the willingness to open and expand out: these compose the foundation on which compassion can grow. To create this foundation is simple, but not easy. Those who have tried mindfulness practice are usually impressed by how difficult it is. We tend to skip to the future or the past. By practicing coming back to the present moment, we can become more adept at paying attention to what is before us.

Just as on the mat there is more satisfaction when my partner is in the moment with me rather than mentally already at the end of the throw, so too in daily life, the more I am present in the moment, the more satisfaction I experience. The more we practice being present, the more familiar it becomes. "The present," I sometimes joke, "is an acquired taste." That is, the more you taste it, the more you appreciate it. It is possible to have a choice whether to think about the future or the past. We can stay focused in the present, attending to the tasks that are in front of us, or we can take a mental journey. We can wander down a road from the past or run through a field from the future, always able to return home, back to the present moment.

Our ability to return home is based on discipline. Discipline is the backbone of practice. And practice is repetition, doing something again and again, until we have a familiarity with, a confidence about, and an ease with the situation. Discipline cultivates the strength to produce a more generous, compassionate way of life.

## PRACTICING LOVING KINDNESS

There are many ways that a person can practice loving kindness. My friend and meditation teacher Sharon Salsberg wrote a wonderful book called *Lovingkindness: The Revolutionary Art of Happiness* about her experience with and development of this quality through the Buddhist practice of *metta*, which I mentioned at the beginning of this chapter.[8] The traditional practice involves repeating a phrase such as *May I be happy, may I be peaceful, may I be filled with love.* Variations of this practice include substituting the names of loved ones or enemies or any or all groups of people or animals. It is the person's repetition of the phrase that cultivates a very strong affection, or devotional quality, that empowers the ideas and feelings of happiness, peace, and love as a genuine part of his or her emotional makeup.

In the beginning of this chapter, I described how important *metta* was for me at a difficult point in my life. And for many years, I have found *metta* to be an invaluable source of strength and support when the more shadowy areas of my psyche begin to overwhelm my thought processes. I have modified the phrase to fit my personal need for emotional balance. For instance, I say to myself, *May I be happy so that I can spread happiness; may I be peaceful so that I can spread peace; may I be filled with love so that I can spread love.* Then I imagine my children smiling and surrounded by light, and I say, *May they be happy, peaceful, and filled with love. May they learn whatever lessons they need to learn as easily as possible.* Then, *May all beings be happy, peaceful, and filled with love.*

Throughout the years, I have heard quite a few versions of *metta,* but for me the important aspect of *metta* is the repetition. There have been days when I must have repeated my phrase a thousand times. I am so thankful to have something to repeat that has a positive quality, that can act as an antidote to the anger, guilt, and shame that invade my mental processes. I sometimes say that *metta* has saved my life. More accurately, it has given me a more loving view of life: it has salvaged my loving side. As I said before, when I first started working with the practice, it took months before felt a shift in my outlook. Self-cultivation—the development of any aspect of ourselves—doesn't happen overnight.

I have been influenced and inspired by Mother Teresa. She was a well-known advocate of compassion. Her specialty was the poorest of the poor. She had a tireless commitment to serving the poor, and much of her sustenance came from repetition as well. Every morning, she began her day with mass. The prayers and gestures of the service empowered her with the faith and inspiration to work long hours in service to the poor. When she won the Nobel Peace Prize, she used the Prayer of St. Francis as her acceptance speech. The repetition of positive phrases can have an amazingly powerful effect on our lives.

## WORKING WITH PRAYER

Because St. Francis of Assisi loved animals and nature, I love his story and his famous prayer. I have found that the prayer works beautifully with a Tibetan Buddhist practice called *tonglen,* which means "giving and receiving." What is remarkable about the *tonglen* practice is that it suggests that we receive negative energy and give out positive energy by breathing in the negative and breathing out the positive. At first, I felt overwhelmed by breathing in negative energy, because I could imagine the negativity. Then I hit upon the idea of integrating the Prayer of St. Francis and *tonglen,* synchronizing my breathing with the phrases of the prayer. The Prayer of St. Francis follows. I breathe in the negative quality where it says "(inhale)," and I breathe out the positive quality, imagining that it radiates in all directions, where it says "(long exhale)."

> Lord, make me an instrument
> of thy peace . . .
> where there is hatred (inhale),
> let me sow love (long exhale);
> where there is injury (inhale), pardon (long exhale);
> where there is doubt (inhale), faith (long exhale);
> where there is despair (inhale), hope (long exhale);
> where there is darkness (inhale), light (long exhale);
> where there is sadness (inhale), joy (long exhale).
> O Divine Master,
> grant that I may not
> so much seek to be consoled (inhale)
> as to console (long exhale);
> to be understood (inhale)

as to understand (long exhale);
to be loved (inhale) as to love (long exhale); (inhale)
for it is in giving (long exhale)
that we receive (inhale);
it is in pardoning (long exhale)
that we are pardoned (inhale);
and it is in dying (long exhale)
that we are born (inhale)
to eternal life (long exhale).[9]

Concentrating on these thoughts and feelings as I take long, rhythmic breaths often puts me in a state of calm acceptance. Doing the exercise, I breathe in and accept those very qualities and feelings that I usually try to resist. Not only do I stop fighting and fearing those parts of myself, I find that I have a reservoir from which I can give positive energy out to others and the world around me. Breathing out positive qualities does not deplete me: quite the contrary, it seems to revitalize me. Instead of trying to protect myself, I can open myself to whatever is there. I was amazed to find that I could easily handle both sides, the shadow and the light.

## REDUCING THE POWER OF OUR FEARS

In aikido, when I am attacked, I attempt to open and take it in. To "take it in" means "to blend with it, accept it, and be with it." Then I guide it out, away from me, and, ideally, the attack is resolved in the positive energy of a throw or a pin and ends in a feeling of well-being for both myself and my training partner.

When we are not struggling with our fears, we have much more energy to apply to compassionate activities. By facing our fears again and again, little by little, we reduce their power. This is why I appreciate the encounters on the mat that trigger my fear. Each time that I face a partner who feels threatening, I can practice opening instead of contracting. The goal is unconditional love. As my compassion grows, my fear diminishes. When we are very young, a tree or a room can seem so huge. When we see it years later, after we have grown up, the tree or room seems normal size, even a bit on the small side. So, too, our fears can seem to shrink if we can mature emotionally and face what it is that keeps us from opening our hearts to ourselves and the world.

春風以接人
秋霜以自肅

*part two*

---

REFINEMENT

*chapter five*

# CULTIVATING VIRTUE:
# INNER STILLNESS

*As human beings, our greatness lies not so much in being able to remake the world—that is the myth of the "atomic age"—as in being able to remake ourselves.*

—Mahatma Gandhi, quoted in Eknath Easwaran,
*The Compassionate Universe*

## SHUGYO

I had been practicing aikido for about six months. On Saturday mornings I would drive into San Francisco for class. One morning our teacher brought a photo of the founder of aikido, Morihei Ueshiba. This was my first exposure to O'Sensei. Aikido classes begin and end with a bowing ritual, which is a statement of respect toward the tradition and the founder of aikido. We were training in a makeshift dojo in the chapel of the Unitarian-Universalist Church at the time, and we usually bowed toward a window with some stacked chairs in front of it. On this morning, there was a photo of O'Sensei propped in the chairs. After class, I asked who this man in the photo was. I was told that he was the founder of aikido.

To my eyes, there was an ancient feeling about him. I asked how long ago he had lived and was told that he had died in 1969, only two years before I began attending aikido classes. Seeing his photo left a deep impression on me. I had an intuitive sense that this man had achieved an extraordinary state of virtue. He seemed to combine tremendous power and deep compassion. I could sense that many years of commitment had developed a depth in him from which virtuous actions sprang unimpeded. The more I learned about him, the more my first intuitive impression was confirmed. His life was a continuous path of self-cultivation, the fruition of which was his ability to embody the statement, "*Budo* is love." This ability is virtue. It is the complete embodiment of a way of life dedicated to love, even in the most difficult of circumstances.

*Shugyo* (pronounced *shoo-giyo*) is a Japanese word that means "self-cultivation," "self-development," or "training." It implies that training in any kind of practice includes the totality of a person's being: the body, the mind, and the spirit. Training encourages the refinement of the human personality and spirit, as well physical presence. *Shugyo* could be understood as the manifestation of the intention to embody a state of virtue.

## THE FOUNDATION OF VIRTUE

Virtue cannot be cultivated directly. Rather, it is the result of growth. More specifically, it is the result of the development and refinement of etiquette, morality, and compassion. There is no substitute for experience. As we train, appropriate responses become grounded and develop into familiar behavior. This form produces both etiquette and an alignment with ethical principles. As we deepen this alignment, moral commitment emerges organically. This is the foundation of virtue. It is the result of a cognitive process, and it also includes a deeper, more intuitive sense of mature generosity. This development of virtue is embodied in a wisdom and a depth that can handle disappointments and accomplishments with equal grace and dignity.

Aikido training offers a way of self-cultivation, of *shugyo*. It is training that relates to the whole person. Self-cultivation training can allow us to realign ourselves with our moral intentions as well as revitalize our bodies. My teacher Saotome Sensei told me, "*Shugyo* is innovation, creativity. Innovation is very important: it is making a new life image."[1]

Many times, students tell me that they feel better after a practice session. Often they report that they feel more connected to their life force, their aliveness. At other times a student will report feeling frustrated. This also is an important part of the training, for only by discovering our limitations can we explore ways to grow beyond them. Through practice, we can discover alternatives to our resistance. As we uncover our courage and integrity, we find the strength to move beyond our sense of limitation. We can see the patterns that keep us in a state of defensiveness, patterns that isolate us and convince us that we must protect ourselves. Seeing this is not pleasant, but it does clarify for us where we must focus our attention.

## RELAXING UNDER PRESSURE

*Shugyo*—that is, training of the whole person—can give us a way to relax our minds as well as our bodies. It can encourage us to open our hearts and act from a sense of connectedness. If this feels impossible in the moment, then we can at least recognize and honor the fact that we are stuck. I have found that acknowledging places where I have become stuck in my practice helps me to recognize that I act out the same patterns in my daily life. If I can see the impasse without panicking, then the correction becomes obvious without any particular effort on my part. Training has taught me that when I relax, I am more powerful, and natural, simple, and compassionate responses can spontaneously move through me.

Ah, to relax under pressure. What a magnificent idea! The question is, How can I actually do this simple but very difficult practice? Training helps me to learn how. Naturally, I prefer not to become stuck, but there is a tremendous amount of information to be found in those moments of stuckness. I can observe that when my body feels resistance, my mind locks onto the resistance, which actually feeds the resistance. Through aikido practice, I have learned that I can expand my awareness. I can allow my mind and body to open up, resulting in a softening of my whole being.

When we were babies, we were more pure in our responses to each experience that came before us. All of us know how strong the grip of an infant is and how magnetically powerful babies are. Now, as adults, we can experience the same phenomenon through an act of recognition that involves relaxing and settling back. A calm and settled state allows a natural, organic power to move through us without interference from our mental agenda or biases. It is exciting and inspiring to find that we still have access to the spontaneous and creative life force that we had as babies.

## TRAINING

Training makes it possible to manifest a spontaneous and creative life force even in difficult situations. Sages and masters have always insisted that daily practice is necessary if we are to clear our minds. And clearing our minds seems especially important in dealing with the frantic pace of contemporary existence. Training helps us to awaken or remember our original nature. We can re-enter the Garden, aware of the apple and the desires and needs that it implies. Training allows us to see our aggression and fear, so that we can then begin to examine them. Tracing our aggression and fear back to their roots allows us to begin at the beginning. When we look at the roots, we can examine how the patterns affect our daily behavior. In practice we have the opportunity to face these patterns and train ourselves in alternatives to unskillful responses. If we do so, soon we will experience the benefits of our practice. Flexibility and confidence will develop. Even in stressful circumstances we will respond with more wisdom and compassion.

The practice of self-cultivation, or *shugyo,* is a rigorous one. Not necessarily physically rigorous, although that could be an aspect of the training, but rigorous in the sense of focused concentration. In Carlos Castañeda's books, which depict altered states of reality, he uses the term "impeccability" in the sense of a person being completely conscious of every activity that he or she performs. He speaks of the necessity of cultivating impeccability in order to become a true warrior. Just as a river continually purifies the water through its movement, so must we continually clear ourselves through practice. If the flow of a river stops and the water sits in pools, then the water will become stagnant and poisonous. Likewise, our systems begin to stagnate and negative thoughts begin to collect when we neglect our practice. Practice is self-cultivation and it enlivens the spirit.

I once asked Takeda Sensei, a master aikido teacher, how someone could develop if he or she was not able to practice the physically vigorous style of formal aikido. His response was,

We already have strength. What we need to do is notice it inside ourselves. If you throw away your desire to be strong, then you can be more natural. If you harmonize with others, if you don't think how to attract him or her, then you can find your own strength already. To develop without strong physical practice takes a strong will, a willingness, and patience. It will take more time. Through exposure to the ideas and the feelings, one can develop this, because it is a capacity that humans innately have. One needs to be reminded of the feeling. Because this connection between individuals and the larger universe exists for everybody, sometimes all it takes is a hint or a word or something that can set up a resonance. Anything that can set up a resonance can cause a large change or an unfolding to happen. This can open a door or create a whole new view of the world.[2]

The confidence that Takeda Sensei has in the human spirit is inspiring. His emphasis on being natural supports my belief that we contain all that we need in order for happiness and freedom to surface. But this doesn't happen without effort. We can allow happiness and freedom to surface in our lives, but only if we make practice, *shugyo*, a priority.

It is possible for a person to develop a way of life in which self-cultivation practices are a regular, normal part of the day. Just as a person brushes his or her teeth regularly, so meditation and breathing practice, as well as physical movement, such as yoga, stretching, or aikido, can be incorporated into his or her daily schedule. It would be interesting for a person to notice what happens to his or her ethics as a result of this kind of integrated training. Would his or her moral view of life begin to shift? Would the desire for a more compassionate heart increase? Would he or she be attracted to ethical refinement or virtuous behavior? These are questions that can be answered only through personal experience. It is important that a person not take anyone's word for it, but that a person find out for himself or herself.

## BREATH

"Respiration," O'Sensei once commented in a lecture, "is the driving force of life. This is the power of *kokyu*."[3] The Japanese word *kokyu* (pronounced *ko-cue*) is often translated as "breath." Aikido includes a series of *kokyu*, or breath, throws. The gesture of a *kokyu* throw is usually that of extending both arms while moving the body in a spiral. *Breath*, in this sense, means "the life force," and the breath of life is an expansive, vital force in training. I particularly enjoy *kokyu* throws because the simplicity of the gestures allows me to focus fully on the sensation of the expanding spiral. There are no complex hand changes or fancy footwork, just the simple, yet profound, spiral expanding outward into the universe. Breath and energy are inextricably linked. One way to focus energy is through the breath. Just as a laser focuses light, becoming a powerful tool, so our concentration and our breath can be used to focus our energy into a clear, compelling force.

In our daily lives, one of the most accessible reference points for the present moment is the breath. Breath is the essence of physical life. It nourishes and affects all aspects of existence. Breath enriches and supports the nervous system, the circulation, and the blood flow. By cultivating qualities in our breathing, we can affect our emotions and our concentration in a positive way.

The inhalation is connected to the sympathetic nervous system. If a person takes three sharp inhalations, then the body automatically goes into a state of alarm, triggering the fight or flight reaction. Blood and energy leave the core and flow out into the extremities—the arms and legs—and ready the body for a burst of activity, ready to fight or run. Conversely, one long exhalation, particularly if the person thinks of it as flowing down or out in a soft, expansive way, ignites the parasympathetic nervous system, which triggers the relaxation response. The blood flows back into the organs, heart, and digestive area and continues to energize and renew the cells within the core of the body and the organs.

In order for the body to be healthy, it is constantly cleaning and renewing itself by cycling through both the sympathetic nervous system and parasympathetic nervous system. The body is designed to handle stress. The sympathetic nervous system automatically responds to the perceived need to take some action. A person also needs to rest and allow the parasympathetic system to kick in and impart a feeling of calm and relaxation.

It is not uncommon, in this fast-paced age, for a person to live in a state of nearly constant stress. Even when there is no physical threat, he or she is so much in the habit of feeling threatened that the sympathetic nervous system is continually triggered. Research shows that when this happens and the parasympathetic nervous system does not have a chance to take over, the immune system begins to lose its strength and effectiveness. A weak immune system is one of the leading causes of disease. In order to keep the immune system healthy, the parasympathetic nervous system must be triggered so that the natural cycle can complete itself.

The good news is that by developing disciplined breathing practices, a person can actually trigger the parasympathetic nervous system. If a person's life is particularly stressful, then he or she can practice the breathing patterns that encourage the calm, relaxed part of the process to emerge. I believe that it is unnecessary to spend a long period in rest time, but a person should train himself or herself to use the breath to relax. Whenever I can remember, I extend the length of an exhalation, allowing the breath to flow down my body, and relaxing my jaw, shoulders, belly, and hips. Usually, after just two or three exhalations, there is a shift in my energy: I feel that there is more time and space to deal with whatever is before me.

Sometimes I actually can see the situation differently. I may realize that there are other alternatives or possibilities in the situation that I hadn't noticed before because there was too much tension in my system. As I relax, I open up a bit, and that sense of openness allows for more options and more flexibility. A new perspective or insight may surface because my mind is not as tense or crowded as it is when I become narrowly focused on a thought or problem.

The general rule in this breathing practice is that the exhalation should be twice as long as the inhalation. I find it helpful to imagine the breath flowing all the way down through my torso, softening and relaxing all my muscles as it travels toward the earth. I usually imagine the inhalation flowing up into my body, renewing and strengthening my muscles and bones.

Another visualization that I enjoy is to imagine that all the bones in my body have a hollow core of light. When I exhale, a warm, liquid light flows down and out through the center of my bones, bringing soft, healing energy through my entire skeletal system. When I inhale, the same liquid light flows up and into my bones, this time bringing with it new, electrically charged particles of light, which enhance vitality and brightness and strengthen my whole being from the inside out.

The combination of breathing long exhalations and visualizing can make a very definite shift in a person's energetic experiences. I am not suggesting that a person can stay in that calm, alive place, but he or she can return to it time and again, achieving a healthier balance between moments of stress and moments of calm.

Breath techniques are a wonderfully simple and easy way to release tension and enhance circulation and flexibility. By practicing long exhalations again and again, a person can develop the habit of calming down. Of course, daily stimulation continually causes energy to rush up and into the chest, neck, and head, but a person trained in breath techniques can respond immediately to that stimulation with a breath, creating a fluid balance between excitement and relaxation.

I always begin aikido and Conscious Embodiment classes with breathing exercises. In any centering process, I usually focus my attention first on the breath. When I am swimming laps in a pool and I lose the rhythm of my breath, my stroke becomes uneven. When I regain the smoothness of my breath, my stroke evens out. At the ocean, the waves along the shore seem to be moving in and out like breath. I sometimes feel as if the surge in the surf is the ocean breathing. It is possible to perceive the breath of life (or breath as life) in all things.

## STILLNESS

I have always loved reflecting water. There is something about still water reflecting the environment—the land and the sky—that momentarily stills my mind and, with it, my body. The stillness brings me into the present moment, suspending mental activity and physical restlessness. With my mind and my body both at rest, my whole being can apprehend the beauty and richness of the moment.

I get the same feeling in aikido when I perceive the still core at the center of the person who is being attacked. Saotome Sensei has the most beautiful example of a still core that I have ever seen. I love to watch how his movement arises out of his core and fills the room. It is like ripples in the water: ever-widening, concentric circles flowing out of the stillness. This sense of stillness within the movement is a mark of maturity in self-cultivation. It takes a very strong center to maintain such a level of repose in the intensity of practice.

This ability to be still speaks of a certain sense of freedom. The stillness that I am referring to is not the repressed type. The admonishment to a child, "Be still! Don't fidget!" creates tension and claustrophobia in that child. The kind of stillness that I mean has an airy, spacious feeling. It allows an appreciation of the richness and textures of life. In stillness, we notice the bees, the light, and the wind. We are aware of birds flitting here and there, tiny bugs crawling busily, and the elfin quality of spiderwebs catching the light. When we are able to be still, the world comes alive.

I once asked Saotome Sensei how he was able to execute a particular technique: he could throw any of us, without any apparent movement, from a wrist grab. He said, "I wait until I can feel your heart beating, and then I synchronize my heart with yours."[4] What a remarkable thing that, in the middle of a training situation, he could be still enough, sensitive enough, to perceive someone's heart beating!

## SEEING FROM ANOTHER POINT OF VIEW

Workplace life and domestic life can be enhanced by a still center point that is able to see situations from a larger perspective. This, of course, requires that a person have the discipline to withdraw from the soap opera of daily existence. True stillness means that a person tolerates feelings of frustration, sadness, or joy without being swept away or allowing the feelings to bias his or her reactions. It provides a little room around the feelings so that a person can receive information from the sensations and keep them in perspective.

If a person's coworker, for example, behaves inappropriately, then the first person can shift his or her attention back to himself or herself. The first person can, energetically speaking, disengage from the emotional flow of the second person's energy. If the first person can become still, then he or she can understand the motivation of the second. This understanding makes it easier for the first person to work with or redirect the second person's intention.

Aikido gives us a chance to investigate experientially this idea of seeing the situation from the other person's point of view. So, too, does Conscious Embodiment. In what I call the *irimi* (pronounced *ir-ree-mee*), or entering exercise, partners stand before each other in stances that represent opposition. Then one person moves behind the other so that both are facing the same direction, and the person who moved can see what his or her partner is seeing. From this position, which acknowledges the other person's point of view, it is easier to lead the situation to a positive resolution. In aikido, the simulated attack may be fast and intense, and the technique may be quick and strong, but the feeling of positive resolution is also present.

## LEARNING TO BE EFFECTIVE

Learning to be effective in physically intense situations gives us the confidence that we can be the same way in a personal, social, or business setting. When we become still and observe in a way that is able to tolerate feelings, we accept others. I have experienced moments in aikido when I could feel a stillness inside myself that became a center, like the eye of a hurricane, while my partner whirled around me with great speed and power. These are moments of beauty and sweetness. The combination of speed, power, intensity, and stillness is attractive, and to be able to stand in the middle of it all and enjoy the feeling is an exquisite gift.

Most people who act in an aggressive way do so because they don't feel understood or accepted. As frustration and discomfort increase, some people feel that if they become more forceful, then they will be heard or respected. In some cases, people may think that by being forceful, they can convince the other person to agree with them.

Occasionally, some people become so forceful that, by overpowering or dominating others, they actually do get their way. Forceful people may have be a momentary sense of victory in this, but in the long run, there is no real feeling of satisfaction. There is no sense of freedom, because the territory, having been established by force, now has to be maintained or defended constantly. This kind of vigilance has a tension akin to that of high-power electric wires. We recognize both as dangerous. This is a very different feeling than the one that comes from a reservoir of stillness, where there is room to breathe and smile, and where one person can appreciate another person's point of view and negotiate with him or her for an equitable resolution.

## CULTIVATING STILLNESS

Eastern meditative practices such as Japanese Zen use the practice of sitting still, being present in the moment, and returning the mind to the still point as a way of cultivating and accumulating virtue. William Johnston says the following in his book *The Still Point,* a study of Eastern and Western mystics:

> Japanese thought has less of the Greek cataloguing of virtues and vices. Though there were some virtues (detachment, poverty, endurance, and patience in adversity) that the ancients loved and admired, the idea of pondering on them and praying to God to inculcate them is not found in Japan. Yet the masters, after practicing their silent Zen, turned out good, virtuous men, as anyone who has met them will testify. That is to say, they emptied the mind of thoughts and concepts, remained in silent emptiness, and this tranquil passivity gave birth to deep virtue.[5]

According to Johnston, the key to advancement along the mystical path is detachment, being able to withdraw all of the faculties into the core of the being, which disengages a person from external events. This capacity for detachment gives the person a wider perspective on the situation. It is not necessary to stay in the stillness, but the willingness to return to it strengthens the ability to sustain this quality.

Cultivating stillness is not always easy. When I worked with women in prison, I discovered that rarely could they stop and be away from the demands of institutional living. The women lived two, three, or four to a cell; the only time that they had their own cell was when they were in solitary confinement. But it was an inspiration to see how they were willing to find ways to create moments of stillness. They would report how helpful it was to stop, become still, and focus, even for a short period of time. They would report that the pauses reminded them to be in the moment. Instead of being frustrated about something from the past or anxious about something in the future, they could be just where they were, in the present, with dignity and integrity.

I was inspired by the courage and commitment that these women showed in the way they continued to practice in an environment that was not conducive to focused, internal practice. Many times I thought to myself, *If these women can practice in such difficult circumstances, then surely I, with all my privileges, can deepen my practice.*

By practicing certain physical and mental attentional exercises, we can build the ability to find the stillness in the space that gives us the freedom to relate to the situation without being caught up in it. This space allows our perceptions to open, so that we can see a greater range of possibilities and make a more informed choice. Our moral integrity can develop, which can lead to the development of compassion. To be still without becoming distracted is a deep and powerful practice. The virtue lies in the depth of cultivation.

## MOMENTS OF STILLNESS

Before the bowing ritual at the beginning and end of aikido class, we sit in stillness for a moment or two. It seems an important aspect of the training. Sitting at the beginning gives us time to gather and focus our energy. We are aware of the stillness of the moment, and anticipate the interactions. I have always enjoyed that "about to" experience. Without the stillness, I can't appreciate the intensity and quality of our readiness. Stopping also provides us with an opportunity to reduce the speed, the sense of rushing. When there is less speed, there is less aggression and a greater ability to be open and receive information.

At the end of class, we again sit in stillness before our final ritual bow. This sitting has a different quality. Usually, a lot of energy and intensity is still flowing through our bodies. As we sit and our breathing and energy begin to settle, the stillness enables us to be in the moment with our bodies, our breath. We have a satisfying sense of having exerted ourselves.

According to Taisen Deshimaru, author of *The Zen Way to the Martial Arts*, "An action cannot be right unless a meditation has gone before it, and coexists with it. Only then can there be true freedom."[6]

## THREE LEVELS OF PRACTICE

There are many ways to develop a certain capacity. I have found that practice can be done on three different levels. The first level is that of ritual, or organized discipline; that is, a specific time and place is set aside for the purpose of focusing the mind in a particular way. For example, I sit in meditation for an hour in the morning. It took me a number of years to build up to that amount of time. Fifteen minutes is a good amount of time for someone to start with. If, however, a person finds that overwhelming, then he or she can start with whatever is manageable.

The idea of meditation is to keep returning the mind and attention to an anchor. The anchor can be the sensation of breath, a posture, a word or phrase, or an image. A person can experiment and find out which of these allows him or her to focus best. The idea is to keep returning the mind to the anchor, gently but firmly. A person should not try to hold the mind there: it will wander. The idea is to keep returning it to the focal point.

This practice develops a kind of attentional muscle, so that the mind doesn't feel either sloppy or excited. The idea is to not follow the train of thoughts and get caught up in their drama. Sometimes the mind is more relaxed and returns to the object of concentration more easily. At other times, the mind is wild and unruly and it struggles. The mind simply "runs away" and gets caught up in the soap opera of dialogue, images, and sensations. There are also moments when the mind can "space out": a person can realize, with a start, that he or she has been inattentive.

All of these experiences are part of the process and path of developing concentration. They are neither good nor bad: they just are, and they are parts of the whole. Just as compost, fruit and flower, decay and death, and fallow periods are all part of a garden's cycle of growth, so our minds have a wide range of experiences that are all part of who we are. During meditation, we have the opportunity to notice our mental tendencies, accept them, and return to our focus point. If we can do this while we are alone, then we have a much better chance of accomplishing the same thing with a coworker or with a family member. It is this capacity that is the foundation of a calm place inside. It is the first level of the process of developing a still point.

The second level of practice is to weave practice moments into our daily lives. Sitting at a stoplight is classic practice time. This time can be used to remember the breath, the posture, a word or phrase, or the visualization; it is another opportunity to return the attention to the present. We can also pause at the moment that we turn off the car. Instead of just jumping out, we can first stop, wait, breathe, and return to that place inside. In the workplace, we can pause for thirty seconds before or after a coffee break or lunch.

Of course, each person must create a form that works for him or her, but with a little intention, it is usually possible to find regular times during the day to pause and withdraw to the concentration point. There is no need to close the eyes or sit or stand in any particular way. From any position at all, it is possible to pause and remember the breath and return to center. And each time we do this, our ability to do it grows stronger, and the calm, still place inside becomes stronger as well.

The third level is spontaneous practice: we practice at any random moment during the day or night. At this level, we keep returning into ourselves so that it is a natural part of who we are. Of course, our attention is constantly pulled out by the events of the day, but we can continuously and spontaneously remember to touch back inside. When we are driving, we are constantly making corrections; it appears as if we are going straight, but we are actually constantly adjusting the wheel. So, too, with attention. We can assume the appearance of calmness and poise that is actually the result of continuous adjustments to the mental pushes and pulls of our inner and outer lives.

These levels of practice have no set time limits. There is no particular amount of time to spend on a level of practice. However, as the years go by, the practice naturally starts to shift. Sometimes, we are influenced by a particular teaching or inspired by an experience, or we come to see the focal point through a different lens. My experience is that it is natural that the practice grows, changes, shifts. It is the principle that is important, the principle of returning attention back to the center. The idea is to be able to withdraw from the drama without disassociating ourselves from it; to stop and look at it without being caught up in its intensity. Even though these calm moments may not last very long, the brief time we spend there is often enough to allow us to gather information, so that we can take or avoid action in ways that are both skillful and compassionate. Cultivating a calm place within ourselves gives birth to inner clarity. It is like water: if it is not stirred up, then it becomes clear.

There is also a possibility of increased contentment if we are able to behave in ways that are more reasonable and less reactive. When we have a sense of the still point, even if our minds get a little "weird" or we get caught up in the drama now and then, we know that we can return to the calm place inside. And if we can't stay there, we don't need to be frustrated, because we know that we can just keep returning to it. We know this because we have done it so many times: hundreds, thousands, or hundreds of thousands of times. We can relax and keep a sense of humor and wonder.

## CIRCULATION

A moment of stillness can be helpful in countless ways. Once we begin to deal with ourselves, then the next challenge is to examine how we interact with others. Relationships can easily draw us into drama. Energy patterns that began in early childhood, even if they are not useful, continue into our adult lives. In the area of relationship, humor and wonder are helpful allies. These qualities allow an openness, which is a kind of circulation. Circulation is a willingness to allow an energy exchange to flow freely throughout the situation, and it is another interesting way to observe our patterns in relationships.

A student once asked me how to keep someone from invading his space. Once again, aikido provided a laboratory in which to examine this question. In aikido training, if a person tries to keep me out of her space, then I will redouble my efforts to penetrate her defense. The more intense the interaction, the harder I push. At first, I assumed it was my feisty temperament, but as time went on, I saw that this is a common phenomenon. When you try to keep someone out, it makes him or her want to come in. To keep someone from invading your boundaries, you can invite him or her into your space. This invitation is part of the process that cultivates circulation.

Good circulation is one of the essential factors of good health. As I have already discussed, when the breath circulates, the energy moved by the breath has a greater chance of cleaning and balancing itself. When this happens, the body has an increased tendency toward balance, flow, and over-all health. The same principle applies to relationships, either with another person or with the environment.

The physical exercises of aikido provide a person with excellent ways to practice allowing incoming energy to circulate through his or her personal territory. In class, the partner represents incoming energy, manifested in physical movement or pressure. Rather than resisting this energy, a person can learn to open himself or herself to it. Aikido techniques allow a person to accept this energy and release it or redirect it back out. These exercises are performed again and again, so that a person has an opportunity to strengthen the ability to relax and open, allowing an exchange, a circulation, of energy between the person's partners and himself or herself.

Having the opportunity to practice in this way has given me a greater understanding of how I tend to tense and contract when pressure is applied to me or when I imagine that pressure will be applied to me. Through training, I have found that if I can open my mind and body and not resist the flow of energy, then a quality of circulation exists between my partner's energy and myself. This changes the interaction to one of communication, rather than control and dominance.

As always, I see these exchanges as a metaphor for how I interact, socially, emotionally, and intellectually, in my relationships. Practice in the setting of a training place gives me an opportunity to check myself and to get honest feedback, which are difficult to obtain during the drama of interpersonal interactions.

The more we train and practice, the more we tolerate—that is, stay stable and open to—sensations in our bodies and our energy fields, sensations that contain information beyond mere intellectual understanding. We can then develop our capacity to respond instead of react. Being responsive, we can let the energy flow out from us while allowing energy from another person into our territories. This kind of fluid interaction creates a situation that is balanced.

Often we either reject and resist the incoming energy or we collapse and contract away from what we feel is invasive. Energy is, by its very nature, responsive. When we are less afraid, we can notice the responsiveness in our energy exchanges. Responsiveness is circulation. Out of stillness comes a response to what is before us. Little by little, we can be more open and sensitive to whatever we encounter and respond with full hearts.

## FINDING BALANCE

I have always wanted to find an appropriate balance between living in the material world and cultivating a spiritual practice. In the 1960s, I "dropped out" of the modern material world. I lived in a cabin without electricity, cooked on a wood stove, and sewed on a treadle sewing machine. I gave away all my possessions except for three changes of clothing, two books, and my guitar. I spent lots of time walking in the woods. My material life was simple, which left me ample time for contemplation and metaphysical investigation.

The 1970s were a time of merging back into society, and the more I participated in it, the more I collected. More things meant more responsibility and less time for walks in the woods and metaphysical inquiry. These days, I am grateful for my hour of meditation each day and the aikido and Conscious Embodiment classes. There are so many material errands and details that must be attended to in order to maintain a house and a car and all that goes along with living in today's world. But the inquiry continues. How can I have a prosperous life in the material world and be connected with total integrity to a spiritual way of being? Is it possible to relate with the world so that I do not make it my enemy or seduce it into being my lover?

We have a tendency to try to manipulate or control our experiences. We usually fluctuate between rejecting things that we don't like and grasping at or trying to sustain things that we do like. We often lack the ability to see things as they are, to work with a situation without bias. Pride, jealousy, longing, and resentment tend to drive us toward material acquisition. Education and media support the belief that the more we have, the more secure and happy we will be.

The spiritual life implies a renunciation of worldly things. Many of the great saints and gurus radically renounced material things. Gandhi and Mother Teresa advocated a life of simplicity and poverty. Depending on what a person believes is important, either simplicity or material wealth can be his or her way of life. What then is the appropriate balance for each individual?

Albert Einstein seemed sure that money is not the way to greatness or satisfaction. He writes in *The World as I See It:*

> I am absolutely convinced that no wealth in the world can help humanity forward, even in the hands of the most devoted worker in this cause. The example of great and pure characters is the only thing that can produce fine ideas and noble deeds. Money only appeals to selfishness and tempts its owners to abuse it.
>
> Can anyone imagine Moses, Jesus, or Gandhi armed with the money-bags of Carnegie?[7]

Some people choose to limit their experiences in the physical world of money and things in favor of time and attention on the internal world. These people spend time in prayer or contemplation. Some, such as Thoreau, withdraw from society, finding apparent fulfillment in communing with nature. This culture does not lend much support to this approach. Usually, people who withdraw to a more contemplative way of life are considered eccentric. But the riches that they seek are those of the interior life rather than those of the material world. They have limited their movement in the material world. And it seems to me that there is a connection between how much a person thinks that he or she needs and the degree of satisfaction that the person experiences.

If, however, a life of poverty or simplicity is not freely chosen, then the restrictions that come with it can be painful rather than liberating.

If a poor person has a family, then the entire family has limited access to higher education, travel, and artistic and cultural experiences. When this kind of limitation is imposed rather than chosen, it can create a desire for fulfillment in the world of material things. A person may believe that having things will bring security and happiness. Unfortunately, many wealthy people are neither secure nor happy.

What is needed is more awareness and conscious choice in the area of material acquisition. How can we develop a certain discipline regarding how much we think that we need? It takes discipline and courage to need less. The media and advertising have focused on acquiring more: more things, more credentials, and more security. Finding balance means that we need to focus our attention in the opposite direction, to cultivate a reduction of our need for things. The less we have, the less we have to protect. The antidote to complexity is simplicity.

If we can stop and become still, then we might find that there is incredible richness right before us. If we can stop acquiring and just be with what we have for a moment, then we might realize that we have enough; in some cases, more than enough. In order to be free, we must break our habit of wanting. Being present in the moment is one way to break the habit. It is up to us to look within, rather than without, for information on how much we need and what will bring us real and lasting satisfaction.

When I look within, look through the eyes of my commitment to self-cultivation, a different scenario emerges. Self-cultivation and the search for moral rightness encourage me to develop myself in the direction of simplicity and attention to detail. If I can pay attention to the amount of things that I acquire, then I can make more appropriate choices in acquiring things. When I want something, I ask myself, *Do I really need it? Will I be able to use it to enrich my life or will it use me to create more neediness?*

My daily practice helps me to wake up and remember that happiness and freedom come from within. I need to learn to use material things to assist me in living a life of integrity and not let them drag me into a world of desire. When I can remember that all the things that we use in our everyday lives affect other people and the environment, it helps me to wake up. I know that the responsibility for bringing balance back into our culture and encouraging dignity, simplicity, and generosity rests with each one of us.

*chapter six*

# CULTIVATING THE WAY: SURRENDER

*The basic act of surrender does not involve the worship of an exter-*
*nal power. Rather it means working together with inspiration, so that*
*one becomes an open vessel into which knowledge can be poured.*

—Chögyam Trungpa, *Cutting Through Spiritual Materialism*

## SURRENDER

In grammar school, we used to play a game called capture the flag:
one team would try to get a piece of colored cloth away from the other
team. Through a series of strategic moves that involved teamwork,
the team without the flag would corner the team with the flag and
require them to surrender it. Then the roles would reverse. Surrendering the flag represented a kind of loss, and so my association with
the word *surrender* began as an experience associated with loss.

*The American Heritage Dictionary* (second college edition) defines
*surrender* as "to relinquish possession or control of to another because
of demand or compulsion; to give up in favor of another; to give up
or abandon."[1] This definition fits with my childhood experiences. In
our culture, surrender often implies weakness or loss. In wartime,
the side that loses surrenders. In school, the younger children surrender to the older children in games as well as in the realm of dominance on the school grounds.

Yet if we think about what is moving or attractive in a love story, it is usually the point at which the protagonists surrender their love to each other. In fact, most people have a deep longing to surrender to another. In this romantic view of surrender, we gladly give up our territory of "myness" in favor of "ourness," or, in a less healthy scenario, "yourness." We wish to feel less separate. We wish to merge our territory with that of our lover.

## DIFFERING VIEWS OF EGO AND SPIRIT

Although having a lover is specific, love itself is all encompassing. I think that a person's desire to find a lover to whom he or she can surrender is a reflection of the desire to surrender to universal love. In both cases, issues of desire and trust arise. I have felt a desire to completely surrender and at the same time felt a fear of surrendering. I wish to lose myself, and at the same time I am afraid of losing myself. This conflict reflects a division within myself. My ego wants to maintain a separate identity: this is the aspect of myself that feels that merging with another or even with my own original nature is dangerous —the equivalent of annihilation. My spirit knows that I am not separate, so there is nothing to lose in merging with my original nature. My ego tells me that I have an identity as a woman, a mother, a teacher, and a lover, and that all these labels must be maintained. My spirit knows that all these labels are temporary, and that my essence as a reflection of universal love cannot be labeled or taken away.

When I feel resistance to change arise, I can understand that it is my ego's fear of losing its identity: change can be the equivalent of an identity crisis. I recognize that my ego has a right to be afraid. After all this time, it has built up an identity, and suddenly that identity is in jeopardy. My ego has no wish to surrender: it wants Descartes' dualistic security, "I think, therefore I am," the great Western achievement of egohood. My spirit, however, responds to Einstein, whose statement I quoted in Chapter One, "Anarchy": "A human being is part of the whole that we call universe, a part limited in time and space."[2] My spirit is not afraid: it knows that surrender simply affirms my connection to universal love. This split is archetypal and the path of self-cultivation is the process of its resolution.

## THE EGO'S VIEW OF SURRENDER

I find it helpful to examine the question, What is it that my ego wants to surrender to a lover or protect from some potential thief? Is it my heart or my mind or my body? And what is it that my ego hopes to achieve by giving up? In other words, what are the components that make up this sense of identity, this sense of self? On the one hand, I want to give up my territory, and on the other hand, I want to protect it.

When someone is rude to me, my ego feels as though that person has invaded or attacked my territory. When someone compliments me, approving of or admiring me and my territory, my ego feels more at ease. If I have decided that I don't like someone, then I want to keep that person out of my territory. And if I surrender to another, then I might be overwhelmed or annexed into that other person's territory.

## SURRENDER AS EMPOWERMENT

It is possible to surrender and yet retain a sense of individual identity. Training helps us to acknowledge the ego's panic while at the same time centering and opening ourselves. We can work with the possibility that we can either invite someone into our territory or allow his or her territory to surround us in a way that is nonresistant and empowering to all concerned. We can practice keeping a conscious connection to the responsive interweaving of energies without becoming lost in the confusion of "myness" or "yourness." Surrender means not resisting the energy of the moment. Ideally, we surrender the conflict altogether: we give up the struggle and no longer try to protect our territory. The question is, How? How do we stop fighting the other person and protecting ourselves?

The process of self-cultivation shows us ways in which surrender enhances our ability to be strong and open. The ability to surrender to the line of our own moral compass resolves confusion and allows us to move toward our goals unimpeded. Cultivating an inner life that is independent and self-renewing, that connects us to a sense of oneness with all things, involves surrender.

Self-cultivation lets us examine the nature of our personal territory. As we clarify what it is that we are protecting, we can begin to work directly with releasing our attachment to parts of ourselves that are not useful. When we are clearer about who we are, we can begin to address the issue of whether it is appropriate or advantageous to surrender. Perhaps, for example, we are not ready to let go of our attachment to our image of ourselves as strong. There are times when we feel a need to be right and cannot let go of our position.

When I come to an impasse with myself about an issue, I say to myself, *I can't let go of this—yet.* The word "yet" is important, because it keeps the door open to the possibility of surrender in the future. It allows me to accept and surrender to the truth that, at this moment, I am stuck and unable to release my attachment to my ego's position. Respecting my ego's attachment keeps me from fighting myself. The word "yet" implies that if I keep training, then I will eventually be able to find a depth within me where these issues may be resolved.

## SURRENDERING TO A DIFFERENT WAY OF LIFE

Many people can surrender to a Higher Power. But in our modern Western society, surrendering to a person is more suspect. In the 1960s, a plethora of gurus from foreign countries came to the United States to convert the open-minded through the ancient practices of yoga, meditation, chanting, and other esoteric techniques used in

Eastern religions. Unlike churches, which usually require only one day a week from the faithful, these approaches asked followers to spend time every day doing practices. Ashrams and communes, where people lived together for the sole purpose of practicing constantly, were established.

In traditional Christian monasteries, where nuns and monks train in order to surrender their lives to the service of God through the church, some of the people who adopt this way of life are able to genuinely give up their attachment to their previous way of life and surrender to the traditional way of life of a devotee. Others drop out after discovering that surrendering in this case means really giving up everything to the teacher or the tradition. On a more mundane level, when we voluntarily enroll in a class or program, we agree to follow the guidelines that make up the form of the class.

## SURRENDERING TO ETIQUETTE, MORALITY, AND COMPASSION

We started with anarchy. In the socialization process of life, we are taught to surrender to the rules and regulations governing our everyday interactions. When these forms are not adhered to and people start behaving in ways that are disrespectful of others—for example, screaming, or throwing things—the feeling is chaos, is anarchy. In order to prevent anarchy, we create etiquette. We follow rules such as crossing the street when the light turns green and not throwing garbage on a neighbor's lawn. In doing this, we surrender to the etiquette of social convention. In a classroom setting, etiquette requires that students sit quietly and listen to the teacher.

When we consider how this etiquette affects us, we are in the territory of morality. We may have a feeling that what is being addressed is right or wrong. We feel strongly about issues that are connected with our fundamental worldview. As our sense of right and wrong becomes more definite, we begin to surrender to it. But if we lack the refining element of compassion, then we want others to surrender to our moral view as well. We feel that they should see things our way, and that they are wrong if they do not. Without compassion, morality may become tyrannical. Caught in this kind of morality, we try to force others into seeing the situation from our point of view.

Compassion brings a little breathing room to the situation. We can still feel strongly about our view and, at the same time, understand that perhaps others do not share our feelings. We can surrender to the world of diversity. Our sense of morality is expanded by compassion, which increases as we surrender to the vastness of human life. Our appreciation for the richness and mystery of life can balance our judgmental tendencies. I agree with Einstein's perspective on this: "The most beautiful and profound emotion we can experience is the sensation of the mystical. It is the sower of all true science. He to whom this emotion is a stranger, who can no longer wonder and stand rapt in awe, is as good as dead."[3]

The more we deepen in our spiritual development, the more we are able to retain an attitude of openness and compassion even in adverse circumstances. We are able to respond rather than defend, and if our ability to respond is nurtured, then it will grow into virtue. When we have virtue, we no longer need to make an effort to surrender: it occurs naturally, spontaneously. We then have such confidence in the view that life is based on connection and communication that we would not be drawn away or distracted from this view even by the possibilities of fame and fortune.

The confidence and stability of virtue is a state of natural, continuous surrender to the Way in which we surrender to the possibility that we are everything and nothing; that life is difficult and easy, happy and sad, and dark and light. We accept it as it is, open to it, and allow it to unfold before us.

## SURRENDERING TO A TEACHER

Growing up during the 1950s and 1960s, I became aligned with the idea of independence. I can't remember specific instances where I was told or shown that independence was something that I should actively cultivate, but I sensed that in some ways I should stand on my own two feet and not depend on other people. A number of teachers have influenced me in important ways, and my tendency toward independence has always been an interesting and, at times, difficult aspect of my exchanges with them. As I grow older and gain more experience in interacting with different teachers, I am better able to strike a balance between surrender and independence. Although there is no exact formula for how the teacher–student relationship should proceed, it is worth examining the issues that surround this situation.

We can surrender to a teacher on any number of levels. At the most basic level, we agree that this person can make certain decisions about our behavior and our actions. If we have personal contact with him or her, then we trust that this person has enough perspective and wisdom to know what is helpful to, and what is problematic in, our development. Even if we don't agree with the teacher, we put those thoughts and feelings aside and follow his or her instructions, because we have agreed to surrender.

When we surrender to a teacher, there are usually certain practices or techniques involved. The teacher wants us to do things a certain way for a certain amount of time. There are usually specific requirements that we are willing to attempt to fulfill, even if we do not completely agree with them. The key here is respect. Respect can be a superficial form of etiquette, or, if resonance and appreciation are present, it can be a deeper form of interaction. The etiquette of agreement to act respectfully toward each other reaches another level when the respect has been earned and appreciation is present. If we respect a teacher, then we will go along with his or her guidance, even if we are uncomfortable or do not entirely agree with what is being suggested. We may choose to place certain perimeters around the amount of time or energy that we will give to the teacher's requirements, but when we acknowledge a person as our teacher, we agree to surrender a certain amount of our time and attention to this person's directives.

I have often heard students from the Western culture say of a teacher, "I didn't particularly like him, but I learned a tremendous amount from him." Ultimately, the teacher's task is to reflect back, or help a student recover, the wisdom that is already present within him or her. This requires an exchange of energy between the student and the teacher.

Resistance to the teacher implies that the exchange of energy is being impeded. In my own experience, when I feel resistance toward a teacher, it is because that person has a strong effect on me. There is a place in me that is not clear, open, or resolved. If I use my resistance as a signal to look more deeply at my thoughts and feelings, then I usually discover an unresolved internal conflict that is ready to be processed. If I discover an internal conflict and unravel it, then I find the root of my resistance. The issue then becomes whether I can surrender my resistance. If I can surrender it, then the experience gives me greater strength and confidence, enhances my morality and compassion, and deepens my capacity for virtue.

## TEACHERS AS CATALYSTS

Teachers are catalysts. They instigate a process that can allow us to open, grow, and change if we will surrender. Even if the surrender is just a matter of acknowledging our resistance, it can still be a reference point for expansion. As Saotome Sensei explained,

The teacher can help the student build a strong center. The student's individual capacity must be respected; also the character, the individual self, the natural self. This is the idea of respecting individualism. There are no two things that are the same. The teacher must support the individual student's becoming freer to live in their values and respect the student's freedom to be innovative. The students must have space to express themselves.[4]

Here Saotome Sensei speaks to both sides of the situation. In order for the teacher to help the student build a strong center, the student must surrender. At the same time, the teacher also has to surrender by acknowledging the individual qualities of the student.

There is a wide range of possible teacher–student relationships. In an extreme situation, a person might totally surrender to a teacher by becoming his or her personal attendant. The entire focus of a teacher's actions and thoughts would be taking care of the teacher and responding to all of the teacher's needs and requests. This can be a rewarding experience for a student, provided the teacher is firmly established in morality, compassion, and virtue. But if the teacher lacks moral integrity, then the situation can become dangerous and result in a cult.

In the United States, individualism and liberty are a strong part of our national identity. We are, on the whole, suspicious of those who try to control our lives, but in some cases, we are not suspicious enough of gurus or teachers who ask for the unequivocal surrender of our bodies, minds, and souls. It is prudent to take the time to examine the situation from a calm, centered place of stillness, for there are times when such an arrangement can be a beautiful and fulfilling experience of surrender.

## THE RESPONSIBILITY OF TEACHER AND STUDENT

An interesting phenomenon occurs when a teacher desires appreciation from a student. This desire seems to create a reciprocal desire on the part of the student for special treatment. When a teacher has developed enough so that he or she does not have an unconscious need for appreciation, then the student can benefit from the teachings transmitted by the teacher without getting sidetracked or confused by the teacher's personal desires. If the teacher is not able to free himself or herself from this need, then the teacher should at least recognize and acknowledge this need within his or her own process.

Just like a student, a teacher has a responsibility to work with himself or herself constantly. For both teacher and student, there must be a continuing process of self-cultivation and surrender in relationship to the teachings; both must work in terms of that common thread and not the feelings engendered by their personal relationship. When the student has a number of teachers, as in the Western academic system, there is less danger of the student becoming consumed by a teacher's desire. Nonetheless, it is still important for a teacher to be as impeccable as possible in this regard. Even if a teacher spends only just a little time with a student, their time together can make a tremendous difference in that student's life.

## EXPERIENCING THE PRESENCE OF A LIVING TEACHER

When I asked Saotome Sensei if he thought that everyone should have a living teacher, his response was,

> Education is not just standardizing: education is using the standard for expression and cultivating individual expression, too. We have a shared standard, a symbolic meaning: we can share our capacity for innovation and our creative ideas because we share the same roots and symbols."[5]

His response implies that a living teacher can share the principles in a creative, dynamic way, a way that is made available through the physical presence of the teacher.

The intensity as well as the confrontational and the supportive aspects of a living teacher provide a specific kind of connection and development that differs in feeling from learning from a video or a book. I believe that in a learning situation involving the whole person—the mind, the body, and the spirit—it is essential have a direct experience of how the teacher executes certain principles. This comes from experiencing the physical touch of the teacher, or transmission, as it is sometimes called. It is always amazing to me to feel compelling quality in the touch of my teacher, Saotome Sensei. It is a touch that seems to defy resistance because of its fluid quality. This quality must be felt in order for its power to be understood. Once the physical experience has been transmitted, then it is possible to supplement the practice with teachings from memory, books, or videos.

Sometimes a teacher is no longer alive, and instead of personal contact, we have contact with the teachings that he or she has left behind. If I understand Saotome Sensei correctly, teachings have symbolic meanings that resonate within us on more than just an intellectual level. The response to discovering a teaching can create such a strong resonance within us that we automatically begin to work with the practices.

### SURRENDERING TO A TEACHING

I was in college when I first discovered the Tao Te Ching. As I read through the verses, I experienced intense sensations in my body. Some of the verses made me weep, and I could not have told you why or how that occurred. I know that, since that time, it has always been my favorite book. When I first read it, the following phrases from verses 36 and 33 reverberated through my being: "The soft overcomes the hard. / The slow overcomes the fast. / Let your workings remain a mystery"[6] and "Knowing others is intelligence; / knowing yourself is true wisdom."[7] Many years later, I still react in a visceral way to these words.

The philosophy of the Tao Te Ching is that there is a natural, harmonious order within life that is already in place, and that if we stop trying to force our will on things, we, too, will become part of that harmony. When I first encountered the Tao Te Ching, I would read a passage and then contemplate what I had read. Sometimes I would spend time in nature with a particular passage in mind or try to discover what aspect of the Tao was in the setting before me.

When I discovered aikido, which is an art that embodies and manifests the Tao, I was completely enamored of its form and feeling. I realized that it was a way that I could study with my body that which had already so captivated my heart and mind. In this case, I found the teachings and worked with them for some years before I found a form or a teacher.

Practicing a teaching without a teacher requires a deep, internal commitment. When things are unclear or frustrating, there is no one to give support or direction. The practice must be continued in spite of this. This type of commitment can be seen, for example, in a person who runs several times a week for years: the inspiration to continue comes from within. Practice involves repetition, and, after a while, the practice may seem boring or uncomfortable and lead to a weakening of the commitment. But even if the practice is boring or uncomfortable, the person may sense that this practice is important to his or her uncovering or resolving hidden internal conflicts.

When we first discover a teaching, it seems exciting and inspiring. At some point, it becomes hard and frustrating. When negative feelings surface, they create resistance. It is at this point that we must recommit, find a renewed sense of surrendering in order to continue working with the practice. In this case, there is no teacher to encourage us. We need to reach deep into ourselves: deeper than the mind, beyond the heart, into the belly, the root of being, which resonates with the desire to live in the light of unconditional love.

Teachings help us to focus. When we do, our minds stop racing. We can begin to slow down, to find that still place, and notice our thoughts. We can inquire why we are thinking such things: we can begin to investigate ourselves. Teachings can also help us to decipher our feelings about moral issues. They usually offer guidance with regard to tuning the moral compass. Often we know that something is true or right because we feel a strong resonance with it; it is as if the moral compass points due north, and we suddenly feel lined up and moving in the right direction. The next sign that we are on the right track is when we notice feelings of compassion, when we consider more than just ourselves.

A teaching, like a teacher, can be a catalyst, a wake-up call. Usually, its value is seen because we wish to be less stuck, trapped, or weighed down. Teachings illuminate the Way: they are the lights that brighten the path as we journey toward centeredness and freedom.

## SURRENDERING TO INTERNAL CONFLICT

A classic example of internal conflict is when the mind thinks one thing and the heart feels another. When I examine internal conflict using the Conscious Embodiment model, I see myself in terms of three centers. The head center deals with perception; the heart center with containing and expressing emotion; and the belly center with a deeply felt sense of purpose. I use the term *split* to describe conflicts between and among these centers. If I am able to identify the differences of opinion between and among the centers, then I can recognize the precise nature of the conflict, an important first step.

The next step is to accept this truth, to surrender to it. This surrender must be more than a cerebral acknowledgment from the head center. The heart, the feeling center, must surrender as well. Surrender must go deeper still: I have to be able to reach my gut sense if I am to make my surrender complete. This is not easy. The human tendency is to acknowledge conflict on an intellectual level and then try to smooth it over or ignore the deeper, less articulated parts it. I often find that I want to move away from these conflicted feelings. I sometimes think of pleasant future events or replay past ones rather than focus on the precise feelings of discomfort or conflict that are arising in the moment. A willingness to see the conflict clearly means taking the time to tune into each part of myself. First, I have to pay attention to what my head center is thinking, and then focus on my heart, my feeling center, and listen to what it is communicating.

The belly center is often the most difficult to understand. Touching my belly and breathing down toward it helps to awaken the "voice" in this part of myself. This process allows me to have a clearer understanding of the conflict within myself. If I surrender to the truth, then I can move into nonresistance. Nonresistance allows my natural fluidity and connection to life to emerge. The tendency for the physical, energetic system to self-organize brings me to a state of unity, and conflicts find an organic resolution. By not fighting myself, I move toward resolution. The path to not fighting myself is one of recognition and acceptance of the anatomy of my habits of fighting.

## TRUTH BRINGS STRENGTH AND ENERGY

The truth can set us free, but we must surrender to it at the most profound level. We can find strength and energy in the act of surrender. This approach of nonresistance is not an act of weakness. In the twelve-step programs, which have helped many people free themselves from various addictions, the first step is to admit that you have a problem. Only then can the journey to recovery begin.

It takes a moment of stillness to be able to acknowledge and allow the emotional pain; then we can examine the elements that are the major factors of this pain. When we are fighting within ourselves and, at the same time, trying to deal with a conflict external to us, it is hard to achieve a positive resolution. To approach our internal struggle skillfully, we must accept ourselves and have compassion for ourselves. Our compassion allows us to surrender and open our hearts: it allows the pain of the dilemma to be acknowledged. Conflicts are important teachers. They show us where our work is and remind us that we must continue to relate deeply to ourselves so that we can meet the challenges of life with acceptance and with inspiration.

On the aikido mat, I frequently experience conflict. If I am not attentive, then I tend to think that I am having trouble with a technique because my partner is resisting me and therefore creating conflict. I have discovered that, usually, the conflict originates within my own body: I am tensing up. That is, I am using both contractor muscles and extender muscles at the same time, which creates muscular conflict within my body. When my partner feels the tension or conflict in my body, he or she tends to respond with tension as well. If I can surrender to gravity, relax my muscles, and then use just my extender muscles, the situation is likely to resolve itself smoothly and easily. It is the recognition of and a surrender to my internal conflict that can lead me to a satisfying resolution.

## VOLUNTARY SURRENDER

In recent years, the medical profession has taken a great interest in chronic pain. The term "chronic pain" implies a physical pain that neither medication or surgery can cure or arrest. People afflicted with chronic pain must therefore find a way to live with this pain. One technique that has helped many of these patients is mindfulness practice: the patient focuses on the pain, notices it, and works with accepting it or surrendering to it.

The premise is that tensing against chronic pain, or hating it, only increases the discomfort. When there is some breadth and space inside the pain, it becomes more bearable. People who have used this technique report that they still have the pain, but they can also continue to function in their lives. The act of allowing the pain and relaxing at the same time lets the body self-organize so that more circulation can occur. The body can begin to balance itself and, although the discomfort continues, life can still be rich and fulfilling.

This implies that for surrender to have a positive effect, the act of surrendering needs to be voluntary. There has to be a willingness. This creates a positive quality that allows acceptance and aliveness to happen simultaneously. Surrender is a rich concept. *Yin,* or feminine, energy is required. There is an opening up of territory. If we can find a way to make room for the pain, at least we are not fighting with it. The wound is there, but we can teach ourselves to stop pouring salt into it.

Surrender does not mean giving up or not doing anything. There is a tremendous amount to do in the practice of being attentive and sensing if we are being true to ourselves and our moral compass: we have to constantly open ourselves and cultivate our compassion. Obviously, a balance between doing and being, action and stillness, needs to be achieved, but it would seem that, on the whole, cultivating an interest in and a capacity for surrender would be helpful to those who yearn for freedom and happiness.

*chapter seven*

# THE OPEN DOOR
# TO FREEDOM: NONRESISTANCE

*Because light has no voice it does not call to you through its voice.*
*Light invites you over through itself.*

—Takami Jun, quoted in Mikio Shinagawa, *Nothingness*

## A FEELING OF LIQUID FLOW

In my years practicing aikido, the most astounding part of the practice has been when I experience the power of nonresistance. It is one
thing to feel my power being met with an equal or stronger power:
what is amazing, however, is to feel my power being absorbed by a
feeling of liquid flow. I have felt it in my teachers, and I strive for the
same quality in my own technique. When I attack my teachers, I try
to grab or strike with a hard and strong intention. My body expects
to feel a hard and strong response in return. It is always a surprise
when my strength is absorbed by a soft, liquid feeling. The alchemy
melts my aggression and resistance, softening my mind and my body.
Even if the softening occurs only for an instant, in that moment, *every-*
*thing is changed.*

Whether the feeling can be sustained has to do with experience and
maturity within the aikido form. It is important for us to be able to feel
this nonresistance in another. Then we can begin to practice finding
a similar capability within ourselves. Still, even if the experience is

brief, it can leave an impression that encourages a deeper capacity for this phenomenal power. I need to feel it again and again, so that confidence and familiarity begin to grow in my own body.

For nonresistance to have that awe-inspiring quality, it must be wholly integrated throughout the body. A person with a cerebral relationship to nonresistance will never be able to sustain himself or herself in the face of physical aggression. Every cell must participate in the quality of fluid receptivity. When this happens, an attacker can find nothing to attack, because there is no place to perch or put hooks into. Everything flows. In aikido practice, we sometimes say of people who have mastered nonresistance that they have left "no openings," meaning, that they have no resistance and therefore nothing to attack.

## INTERNAL PRACTICES

Nonresistance is cultivated through the internal arts or practices. Aikido and meditation can both be considered internal practices in that we attempt to absorb or accept the energy of a situation instead of defending against, resisting, or rejecting it. External arts tend to emphasize meeting strong power with equal or stronger power. In the internal arts, alchemy happens through the fluid quality of complete receptiveness. When we try to change someone or something, we resist what is. When we can open, however, and accept the situation without any resistance, it changes itself automatically without any effort on our part. For aggression to sustain itself, it needs something to go against. When aggression meets nonresistance, it loses its power.

An innate sense of center and balance is found within the nonresistant state. The focus in both aikido and meditation is on coming into balance and harmony with ourselves. In both forms, we can see the result of resistance and the result of nonresistance. In both forms, it is through the acceptance of resistance that we arrive at nonresistance. As I noted in the "Introduction" to this book, O'Sensei says,

"[Aikido] is not for correcting others, it is for correcting your own mind."[1] In training with our partners, we are not trying to control them: we are trying to control ourselves, open ourselves, and soften ourselves—not a collapsing type of softness but an absorbing softness.

*The American Heritage Dictionary* (second college edition) defines *nonresistance* as "the practice or principle of refusing to resort to force even in defense against violence."[2] Violence does not necessarily mean physical violence: violence can be any perceived threat. When we feel threatened, we tend to react. In my case, when I feel threatened, I tend to become resistant and aggressive. My practice is to first step back from my initial reaction and find a calm, still place inside myself. This allows me to be more responsive and find a way to work with, instead of struggle against, the situation. In nonresistance, the softening and moving with the direction of the situation is not a weakness. It is a positive joining with, an opening to, the energy that is arising. When one stream of energy is accepted by another stream of energy, how can opposition arise? The power of nonresistance is not to impede the power of a force but to open to it, join with it, and redirect it.

## REDIRECTING ENERGY

The ability to redirect energy is one of the essential qualities of leadership. For a person to exercise nonresistance in a truly powerful way and to lead skillfully, he or she must have the background or the bigger picture as a reference point. Sometimes it is impossible to see the bigger picture or to know it cognitively. If so, a person can still have an intuitive grasp of it. He or she can have a sense that the forces driving the situation and the behavior are bigger than he or she can understand in the moment. Sometimes these forces may seem to come from a very old place, a place that feels generational or ancestral. In these times, it is wonderful to be able to refer to our training. We can draw upon the sense of stability that practice gives us, a stability that can match the force of the situation. We can flow with the situation without fear of losing ourselves or being overwhelmed by the whole thing. We can begin to appreciate the intensity and power involved. Martin Luther King Jr. said the following in a speech on loving your enemies:

> We shall match your capacity to inflict suffering by our capacity to endure suffering. We will meet your physical force with soul force. Do to us what you will and we will still love you. . . . But be assured that we'll wear you down by our capacity to suffer, and one day we will win freedom. We will not only win freedom for ourselves; we will so appeal to your heart and conscience that we will win you in the process, and our victory will be a double victory.[3]

The power of nonresistance, so elegantly articulated here by King, is a tremendous resource available to us all. He showed us that leadership and nonresistance can overcome what seem to be impossible odds. But before we can apply nonresistance to outside forces in our lives, we must be able to apply it to ourselves. Through a process of carefully attending to our thoughts, we can examine the places where we struggle with ourselves, where we tense against ourselves. We need to apply the principles of opening, softening, and accepting to those things within ourselves that we want to resist and reject.

## LEVELS OF NONRESISTANCE

Nonresistance can function at many levels. In order to prevent chaos and anarchy, we can function at the etiquette level of nonresistance. We can act nonresistant because it is the polite thing to do, not because we genuinely feel nonresistant. When the desire to actively choose nonresistance arises, we move to the level of nonresistance as morality: we begin to feel the rightness of nonresistance. If we begin to extend this feeling to others, then we become motivated by compassion.

As we gather experience and begin to mature, we feel surer, clearer, and more relaxed about nonresistance: we feel the truth of it. At this point, we have no doubt that nonresistance is our path and that virtue is the result of this realization. We don't have to go against anything: we can simply go forward or go in. There is confidence and open-heartedness. I have experienced this kind of nonresistance on the aikido mat, and it was like entering a pool of warm light. I could not fight because there was nothing to fight against.

When I practice aikido, I usually imagine that my partner is an extension of myself, that my partner and I are two conflicting parts of myself: the person who is attacking me is really me attacking myself. The motto of aikido is "true victory is victory over oneself."[4] When I train, I see if it is possible to move with the incoming energy, and, if not, I study the outcome of my resistance. This helps me begin to understand at a cellular level that resistance doesn't work. Then I can begin to experience at a cellular level how powerful nonresistance can be.

## THE POWER OF THE CIRCLE AND THE TRIANGLE

Nonresistance can be studied in terms of shapes. In aikido, the two shapes that I have worked with most are the circle and the triangle. The circle is more of a feminine shape and implies a sense of territory, a boundary. When we practice nonresistance, others are welcomed into our circle or space: we don't try to keep others out. And because they are not being kept out, these others do not have to be aggressive. The triangle is more of a masculine shape and can penetrate without resistance. In just the same way, a sharp knife can move through even a dense material. A wonderful Chinese poem called "Cutting Up an Ox," by Chuang Tzu and translated by Thomas Merton, illustrates this exquisite ability to penetrate through a dense material when there seems to be no room:

Prince Wan Hui's cook
Was cutting up an ox.
Out went a hand,
Down went a shoulder,
He planted a foot,
He pressed with a knee,
The ox fell apart
With a whisper,
The bright cleaver murmured
Like a gentle wind.
Rhythm! Timing!
Like a sacred dance,
Like "The Mulberry Grove,"
Like ancient harmonies!

"Good work!" the Prince exclaimed,
"Your method is faultless!"
"Method?" said the cook
Laying aside his cleaver,
"What I follow is Tao
Beyond all methods!

"When I first began
To cut up oxen
I would see before me
The whole ox
All in one mass.

"After three years
I no longer saw this mass.
I saw the distinctions.

"But now, I see nothing
With the eye. My whole being
Apprehends.
My senses are idle. The spirit
Free to work without plan
Follows its own instinct
Guided by natural line,
By the secret opening, the hidden space,
My cleaver finds its own way.
I cut through no joint, chop no bone.

"A good cook needs a new chopper
Once a year—he cuts.
A poor cook needs a new one
Every month—he hacks!

"I have used this same cleaver
Nineteen years.
It has cut up
A thousand oxen.
Its edge is as keen
As if newly sharpened.

"There are spaces in the joints;
The blade is thin and keen:
When this thinness
Finds that space

There is all the room you need!
It goes like a breeze!
Hence I have this cleaver nineteen years
As if newly sharpened!

"True, there are sometimes
Tough joints. I feel them coming,
I slow down, I watch closely,
Hold back, barely move the blade,
And whump! the part falls away
Landing like a clod of earth.

"Then I withdraw the blade,
I stand still
And let the joy of the work
Sink in.
I clean the blade
And put it away."

Prince Wan Hui said,
"This is it! My cook has shown me
How I ought to live
My own life!"[5]

The lines "When this thinness / Finds that space / There is all the room you need!" are a beautiful description of the penetrating quality of the triangle, a shape that has the attributes of a blade. The triangular energy or blade easily finds "the secret opening, the hidden space." Within us lies the potential for this level of mastery. With practice we learn to navigate rush hour traffic, busy calendars, or family quarrels. When we are present and not resisting ourselves, we begin to center and relax, and then we can find the way through difficult situations and discover that "There is all the room you need!"

## WORKING WITH SHAPES

We can look at space—the space within something or the space outside of it—from the point of view of boundaries. Boundaries can be examined in geometric shapes. Aikido and many other traditions have used the circle, triangle, and square as a way to relate to and define space and give it meaning. For our purposes, the shape of the space needs to relate to the situation. In other words, if I experience a strong pressure coming toward me, it is helpful to adjust my sense of space so that I can open up. Like the image in the ox story, when I am more relaxed and expansive, I accept the pressure: it meets no resistance.

My great fear—what keeps me from opening up—is that I will be overwhelmed or annihilated. We all have experienced being overwhelmed, and the memory of the discomfort makes us tighten up or close. Through Conscious Embodiment or aikido practice, we can learn to open up without feeling overwhelmed. As we open in a skillful way, we can stay lively and present with our responses and relate as much to the space as to what is entering it.

In aikido, the incoming pressure can be directed within the space into a neutralizing spiral. This is done with a circular or turning technique. Or the energy can be sent on its way in a triangular shape. Opening up allows the partner to move through or past the space, without any collision. Or the incoming energy can be stabilized into a square. In this case, the movement is stopped and the partner is taken down to the mat. As a parent, there were times when I had to say no to pleas for parties or visits from friends on school nights. The more I was squared away around the issue, the less whining and complaining I received.

In order to allow the energy of these shapes to be responsive, we need to explore, practice, and strengthen these different shapes in response to pressure. That is one of the great benefits our training place, our laboratory. We can repeat the experiment again and again until a more visceral, cellular understanding of these shapes begins to take effect and we have more clarity about how the space affects the interaction. Shapes are not about resistance. They allow the energy of the situation to be organized in relation to a particular space.

The circle can be either inclusive or exclusive, depending on whether an issue is, on moral grounds, being accepted or rejected. When I was working at the prison, there were times when the women would complain about one another or the staff. In some cases, I felt able to open my circle of awareness and compassion and accept their opinions as valid from their point of view. Sometimes I felt that their comments were inappropriate, and, rather than accepting them, I was able to say that I neither agreed with nor believed what they were telling me, thus clearly rejecting their ploys to draw me into their arguments. Without excluding them, I was able to hold my own center in the circle of my awareness.

The triangle represents the penetrating aspect of our energy: it defines and refines the direction. The ability to terminate a project or begin a new project has to do with taking action. The capacity to penetrate through hesitation or procrastination and move ourselves forward in a nonresistant way is a wonderful ability, available to us all. With practice, we, too, can be like the cleaver finding its way easily through the tough joint.

The square is about steadfastness and stability. It can provide a container for the intensity of our energy. It teaches us how to be stable and enduring without resisting or struggling with ourselves. It gives us information about staying put and being on the spot.

The shape of the space can have an effect on the way that we perceive time. A large, expansive circle is about acceptance and seems to slow things down. No speed is needed because everything is included. A sharply defined triangle implies penetration and acceleration. We are clear about our direction and we are moving forward. Because nothing impedes us, the movement can be swift. A square can give the sensation of momentarily stopping time altogether. Our moral attitude is that of immovability. Like a stone castle, we will stay in this place for generations: we will not be moved. There is no need to fight, no need to resist: each shape can help us work with the situation just as it is.

## WORKING WITH TEXTURES

The Exploratorium in San Francisco has a building where the public can learn about and experience lasers, light shows, and amazing displays of physics. It also has a tactile dome, where visitors can experience all kinds of textures. In it are substances that are smooth, slimy, or soft; others are hard, rough, or prickly. There are mini-environments, in which visitors can feel heavy or light, or where the air feels thick or thin. Some of these textures may trigger a strong aversion: they may feel gross or disgusting. Some environments may make visitors feel claustrophobic. Other textures or environments, however, may elicit positive feelings: relaxed, open, warm, or cool.

An Exploratorium is a good metaphor for our lives. Experiences can be viewed as textures instead of situations that we resist or that overwhelm us. We may always have certain preferences, but what will help us live more balanced lives is the ability to function in and work with as many kinds of textures as possible. Often when we have preferences, we tend to tighten around them. We tighten to hold onto the experiences that we like, so that we don't lose them. When we do this, we forget that losing them is inevitable, because everything changes.

We also tighten around experiences that we don't like: we tighten to keep them out of our space, we tighten against them. Tightening is a contraction that limits the capacity for freedom of movement. When the system is contracted, there is less flow and less movement. Less flow means less information. And when we have less information, we are not able to respond to the nuances of life. In fact, we may miss some subtle, or not so subtle, changes altogether.

An interesting experiment can give you an experience of this. Take two objects of approximately the same size and shape, one heavier than the other. A tennis ball and a juggling ball or a screwdriver and a hammer will do very well. Hold one in each hand, with your hands and arms relaxed. Feel the difference between their weights. Now begin to squeeze them, and squeeze until you are really tightening all the muscles in your hands and arms. See now if you can still feel the difference between their weights. Usually, the only thing that you can feel is your own muscles squeezing, because you have lost the ability to distinguish the weight differences between the two objects.

In life, we may be squeezing our energy around certain situations. When we do this, we are unable to get information about these situations: we cannot feel their texture. We lose appreciation for the lightness or heaviness of the moment. Nonresistance restores our ability to be sensitive to the nuances of the here and now.

Textures add a rich, sensual quality to our lives. All experiences have integrity and are worthy of respect, just like all plants and animals. We wouldn't think that an orchid is good and a cactus is bad because the cactus is prickly and the orchid is not. We respect the cactus for its texture. We may feel that it is just as beautiful as the orchid, perhaps even more so. In the same way, in life, it behooves us to have respect for and tolerance of the textures of situations. I find it helpful to think of people and experiences in terms of plant metaphors. A person could be prickly or smooth, or, like a rose, beautiful, sweet smelling, and prickly, all at the same time. Like plants, situations can be delicate or strong, huge or tiny.

We can cultivate nonresistance. We can train ourselves to relax and open, to feel and tolerate the textures as they present themselves. When I recognize that I am tense about a situation, one technique that helps me is to tighten even more. I intensify the experience of tightness so that the sensations and consequences become very clear. Then I exhale and release the muscle tension. I can feel the contrast and thus am reminded of the difference between being tight and being relaxed.

If I repeat this a couple of times, then I really start to understand, at a felt level, the difference between tight and loose. The more relaxed, loose state allows more information to come through my system: I am more aware of the textures and intensity that are present. The question is, Can I tolerate this information? As a child, I tightened up because I could not tolerate the information: I couldn't stand some of the textures. Part of my maturing process was becoming able to tolerate textures and to function when I was uncomfortable.

A certain Buddhist practice requires a young monk to sit with a corpse for a specified number of days while it rots. The monk must smell and witness the decomposing of the body. The point of this practice is to help the monk become accustomed to the inevitable process of death and recognize the impermanence of all things. If a person can tolerate such a thing, see the truth without resisting and tensing against it or becoming overwhelmed, then the fear that accompanies the experience begins to lose its power. Accepting the smell and the sight of decomposing flesh is, by our Western standards, a radical practice. Yet this practice could help a person to be calm and relaxed in the face of death—or disease or old age, which, for some people, hold more charge than death itself.

Fear has a texture and it is a sensation, and it is possible to train ourselves to tolerate this texture and this sensation. If we can tolerate fear, open to it, then we can get more information. We can begin to understand and accept that the movement toward old age and death is inevitable. Instead of being afraid and tensing against it, we can face it with the virtues of dignity and integrity. Nonresistance helps us to discover the beauty and richness of the natural, unfolding process.

In the years that I have been practicing aikido, I have experienced many different textures in the exchanges between myself and my training partners. At first, I had strong reactions to different textures of energy. I didn't like certain textures and really enjoyed others. I found myself avoiding certain people and seeking out others. Aikido is an excellent metaphor for life, and I realized that I was repeating this pattern off the mat.

Aikido enabled me to see the pattern for what it was: aversion and desire. I found that, in accordance with Buddhist philosophy, trying to make things different than they are leads to suffering. I would be frustrated and uncomfortable when I found myself working with one of the partners whose texture I didn't like, and I would expend energy trying to secure time with partners who I thought would make me feel good. Once I realized what I was doing to myself, I began the long road toward equanimity. After all these years, I still feel preferences and tendencies. But now I have a greater capacity to experience someone else's energy as an interesting texture. As a result, I have a greater capacity for honesty, clarity, and compassion.

Textures are part of the richness of life. My growing ability to be open to a greater variety of textures has given me faith in my own process. Faith has been key in moments of uncertainty or when the difficulty seemed insurmountable. Faith is an outgrowth of nonresistance, for when we are not fighting or ignoring whatever is before us, we can open ourselves to it and embrace it.

## FAITH AND DOUBT

According to the Bhagavad Gita, "Every creature is born with faith of some kind . . . Human nature is made of faith. Indeed, a person is his faith."[6] I have struggled with doubt for most of my life. Like all behavior and strong emotions, doubt implies its opposite, faith. I have had moments of faith that equaled and surpassed the moments of doubt. When I experience doubt, my system contracts; when faith is present, there is expansiveness. Doubt is shadow, faith is light. They are also located in different parts of my body. Doubt seems to come from my head and seems to be the result of certain thoughts. Sometimes faith feels as though it emanates from my heart, and sometimes I sense its foundation deep in my belly.

If I find myself in a doubting mode, then it helps to recognize that I am in my head. Having acknowledged the thoughts in my head, I can then shift my attention to my heart. Moving my awareness into my heart changes the experience. As my heart opens to the doubt, accepts the doubt, an alchemy begins to take place. It is the alchemy of nonresistance. The doubt, with nothing to resist, is transformed by acceptance to its essential energy form: faith. It seems as though the strength and confidence for this process come from deep within, from my belly. The confidence from this deep place provides the foundation from which my heart can open and embrace the doubt in unconditional acceptance. This is an environment where doubt and faith can coexist and can unfold in a natural, organic way.

## FAITH AND MEANING

Many life experiences are inexplicable. The question children ask most frequently is Why? This "why" implies a need or desire for knowledge, which represents security. Sometimes there are logical explanations, but quite often there are not. Some children seem to know that there is a connecting thread or pattern in the order of things. Others seem less convinced and constantly ask adults for explanations and reassurances about the outcome or meaning of events. For some people, faith is a given; for others, it grows through experience. Faith allows us to move forward when there is no logical truth or material evidence, when we have reached the boundaries of what Takeda Sensei calls the physical mind. It can be present as an intuitive sense or a conditioned belief. A sudden event or incident can awaken a belief in the meaning of existence.

Some people gain a sudden insight into the purpose of existence through a near-death experience, when it becomes obvious that to resist death would be futile. Sometimes they see events in their lives pass before them, as in a movie. Reviewing their lives allows them to see meaning in these events, which encourages them to change their ways, becoming more positive and nonresistant. They see evidence that there is indeed a direction, a moral compass, that must be followed. They understand that their actions, even the incidental ones, have a powerful effect on the lives of those around them. Their compassion is awakened, and they develop a belief in the importance of positive, loving actions.

## FAITH IN A HIGHER POWER

Another kind of faith is the belief in a Higher Power, something greater or divine. The theistic approach says that by nonresistance we can become receptive to, or be a container for, the divine spirit, which enters and imbues our lives with a state of grace. The pantheistic view assumes that all things, including people and creatures, are automatically imbued with divine spirit. The divine spirit is not received: instead, we open to it, we do not resist what is already there. In either case, belief in a divine intelligence can inspire principled behavior that is informed by respect for the interconnection of all things.

If this kind of faith becomes a genuine reference point, then it can inspire mature, responsible behavior. Faith creates a consciousness of the repercussions of our behavior. If we believe in the connection between the human and the divine, then we must admit that our behavior affects that relationship. As a result, we may become more ethical, making an effort to face up to and change our inappropriate and selfish behavior.

## FAITH AND SELFISHNESS

Selfishness is based on the impoverished view that there is not enough and that we must acquire more and more if we are to feel satisfied and safe. In some cases, faith can be an antidote for the selfish lust for more territory, power, and control. This lust is an appetite that can never be satiated because it confuses the desire for union with the divine, the universe, or the Way with the desire for territory. When desire gets out of control, we can lose our perspective: behavior based on lust for personal satisfaction can result in great suffering.

Even if we have strong desires, we can respond to them without becoming selfish, consumed, or swept away. Using nonresistance we can temper them with the ethical quality derived from faith and refined through compassion. We can still find joy and satisfaction in our own accomplishments—and also in the accomplishments of others. Our faith is strengthened when we remember that we are connected to something more than just ourselves. This was the realization that opened the door to personal growth in the first place. The door leads to a more expansive view of who we are and how we fit into life.

## FAITH AND PRACTICE

Once again, it comes back to practice. An effort to cultivate nonresistance leads to faith. Sometimes it feels like the effort is hard work. At other times it is easy, what the Buddhists refer to as effortless effort. Our experiences can lead to insights, and our insights to understanding, but it is only through practice, through discipline, through effort that the understanding can work its way into our cellular selves. Once our cells have experienced the possibility many times, we can relax and enjoy our natural, intuitive responses. Faith, I think, is in all of us. We only have to remember it and cultivate it in our everyday lives.

A garden doesn't grow vegetables on its own. It needs cultivation. When properly attended to, it produces lovely, nourishing food. When left uncultivated, it produces weeds. To cultivate or not: the choice is ours to make. No one forces us to cultivate faith: it is the natural outcome, the virtue, that arises from following our moral compass with compassion. If we wish to do this but cannot, what is it that inhibits us? It's not a force from without but something from within. Our practice of nonresistance gives us the ability to consult our moral compass, open our hearts, and choose the way toward freedom.

*chapter eight*

# TIME, SPACE, AND ENERGY

*Time past and time future*

*What might have been and what has been*

*Point to one end, which is always present.*

—T. S. Eliot, from "Burnt Norton" in *Four Quartets*

## BALANCING TIME, SPACE, AND ENERGY

The elements of time, space, and energy are aspects of every situation. They can either impede or enhance the way that we function. Looking at them in terms of the verses from the Tao, we can associate time with etiquette, space with morality, energy with compassion, and virtue with all three working together in perfect balance. When we are out of balance in any one of the three, the others are affected and the whole situation becomes a struggle instead of a situation where, unlike the situation described in "Cutting Up an Ox": "There is all the room you need! / It goes like a breeze!"[1]

When any one of these elements is not functioning harmoniously, the other two are affected. It does not matter which element we start with. Timing, for instance, can become an issue of speed. One of the things that impedes our ability to accept any incoming force is the feeling that it has too much speed. When things feel as if they are moving too quickly, our sense of space is affected as well. This creates a feeling of too much energy. When we have too much energy, we begin to feel overwhelmed. If we suddenly feel claustrophobic, it will affect our sense of proper timing, our energy level, and our ability to be alert and present in the situation.

As concepts, these ideas are not hard to understand when we are in balance with ourselves. But knowing that these elements—proper etiquette, morality, and compassion—are natural, obvious behaviors is not enough to make us implement them when we are out of balance and feeling pressure. It is through training, through practice, and through perseverance that we can develop good timing, a sense of spaciousness, and a relaxed response to the energy, or intensity, of the situation.

## TIME: ETIQUETTE

Time has an elastic quality: a minute can be a long time and an hour a short time. Speed needs to be appropriate. Etiquette has to do with appropriate responses to the situation. Being able to go slowly with awareness is as important as being able to go quickly safely. When we practice and develop ourselves, we are usually developing good timing: honing our reflexes.

Reflexes are our ability to respond to a situation. Experience can help us develop reflexes that respond in a calm, relaxed way to a situation. The real test is always when we are feeling pressured or when there is danger. How well do our systems respond in these times? Can we have good timing and be appropriate in the circumstances? Knowing when to wait and when to move is the essence of timing. For example, in conversation, do we know when to say something and when to be quiet? Timing can be worked on cognitively, from the point of view of etiquette or appropriate movement, but its refinement seems to come from a deeper place.

Timing seems to be enhanced through relaxation and nonresistance. This sense of roominess allows us to respond to the situation more harmoniously. When timing operates smoothly, our actions seem to move through us effortlessly. This is our creative, intuitive knowing, which operates beyond or before conscious awareness, arising unimpeded to address the situation spontaneously. When I "try" to have good timing, I usually lose some precision, because my conscious mind interferes with the intuitive process. The softness of non-resistance awakens the intuitive response and increases the quality of ease, resulting in good timing.

On the aikido mat, I can feel when my timing is off: my movements lack smoothness and ease. And when I am teaching or watching my students practice, I can see when their timing is off. The interactions look tight, and there is often a jerky, hurried feeling to the interactions.

Moving too late or too early affects the distance—the proper spacing—between partners, resulting in tight muscles. When the muscles tighten, the feeling of tension is obvious, even to those who are observing. When the timing is on, the observers will note ease and fluidity. Repeating a technique again and again allows the body and mind to begin to relax so that appropriate timing will become more automatic.

Awkwardness in social situations is often a matter of timing. In life, when I can tolerate the situation—that is, relax and release my attachment to the outcome without retracting or tensing up—I seem to be able to interact with others without feeling awkward. Appropriate etiquette allows the interaction to proceed with an awareness of the proper intervals within a conversation or exchange. Studying timing on the mat gives me clues as to how to cultivate a better sense of timing in my whole life. The principles are the same: I need to be centered and relaxed in order to intuit the precise moment when or where something should be said or done.

Yet etiquette, precise movement, and proper speed by themselves are not enough for me to a feel totally satisfied. I also need to have an inner motivation, a reason to pursue the situation more deeply. My timing needs direction and a deeper meaning within that direction. When I am relaxed and calm, I have access to the still point, which allows for clarity regarding my moral direction. As I begin to define my moral direction, a sense of spaciousness grows within me.

## SPACE: MORALITY

Space and time interact with each other in such a way that ultimately they are inseparable. We can, however, separate them in order to and look at each element in terms of its impact on a situation. It is interesting to see how different people respond to being attacked. Some freeze, some run away, and some, myself included, fight back. Many aikido practitioners have always tended to fight back, even before they took up aikido.

Habitual response patterns of freezing, running away, or fighting back affect the feeling of space in difficult situations. In Conscious Embodiment classes, we practice slowing down our movements when we are pressured. Because there are no aikido techniques to execute, we can consciously open up, expand our energy, and feel the space in and around our interactions. If a person's typical response pattern is fighting back, then a practice of slowing down and opening up is repeated. In time, slowing down and remaining calm while feeling pressured becomes a genuine possibility. This allows us to be more flexible and responsive in stressful situations. When we are less reactive and more responsive, we can gain access to a deeper level of right action for the moment and our morality is awakened.

Our culture cultivates in us a tendency to fill up the space around us. We sometimes identify with a need for entertainment and are uncomfortable if there is no CD, book, or TV to absorb our attention. Psychologically, we find it difficult to allow a sense of space in our thought processes. The ego, the personal identity, wants to maintain itself. It fills up the space in the thought processes with planning, ruminating, fantasizing, and understanding.

I have found that by concentrating on the space, relating with openness and with the qualities of energy and color in my mental environment, an ability to be in stillness has grown within me. It is a great relief to my psyche when I stop trying to grasp some concept or understand some event. For me, resting in spaciousness is an experience of profound being, and I find great beauty and satisfaction in these moments. I like to think of the mind as being like the sky and the heart like the ocean. In this state, I am not confused about what to do: I have a deep knowing about the rightness of an action.

## ENERGY: COMPASSION

The third part of this triad—energy—informs our feelings and perceptions. Compassion refines our sense of right and wrong by expanding our perimeters of consideration. It takes energy to have compassion, to go beyond the constraints of right and wrong and enlarge our view. This energy of compassion imbues the entire situation with a more expansive view of how we are intrinsically connected to all things.

Energy can be described as vitality, intensity, or the capacity for action. More fundamentally, it is the innate activity of particles vibrating within atoms and molecules. It is vibration. If two energies are vibrating at a different rate, what happens when they meet? Clearly, they will affect each other. We can study chemical reactions, but our interest here is the interpersonal perspective: how we affect each other emotionally, how we handle the intensity. If a strong emotional energy is coming toward us, we may think that it is too much—that we will may overtaken—and thus we may feel threatened.

I often say in Conscious Embodiment classes, "Ask yourself, *On a scale of 1 to 100, how much energy does this situation represent?*" The idea is to begin to train ourselves to recognize the amount of energy in each situation. If we can equalize the amount of energy coming toward us with the same amount of energy coming from us, then the situation will be balanced rather than overwhelming. If we recognize that more is coming toward us than we are comfortable with, then we need to train ourselves to be able to tolerate more intensity coming into our space. When a person behaves in a way that makes us uncomfortable, energy begins building inside of us.

In the practice of aikido, I have felt in myself and watched in others an aggressive response to these feelings of discomfort. Somehow the system feels threatened. This is the point at which it becomes difficult to consider softening and accepting the incoming energy. This is an important metaphor for emotional and psychological situations in which defensiveness impedes the ability to really listen and try to understand another person's behavior. I have learned that I must first be able to tolerate a person's energy before I can really open myself to hear the content of what he or she is expressing. Aikido has helped me to develop the capacity to tolerate someone else's energy.

Tolerance is what allows us to listen in an open-hearted way to what is being said. Whether it is being said through the body, as in aikido practice, or through words and gestures, the principles of balancing and equalizing are the same. The ability to allow feelings of intensity and energy is the basis of genuine compassion. Anyone can be compassionate if the situation is kind and supportive. The real test of our capacity for compassionate action comes when the situation is intense, energetic, or even aggressive.

Understanding the direction or shape of the energy helps us to orient ourselves. The next step is to cultivate the ability to accept and work with energy. If we practice, then we can become fully capable of responding appropriately to a high-intensity situation without being overwhelmed.

## ENERGY, EXPRESSION, AND CONTAINMENT

Within my system are shapes and directions through which energy manifests itself. My spontaneous reaction to intense energy is usually fight or flight. As I progress along the path from anarchy to freedom, a refinement begins to occur. Fight or flight becomes expression or containment. Expression is an expansive, outward flowing of energy. Containment is an inward movement that builds or stores up energy.

Expression implies the ability to allow energy to flow out unimpeded through my system. It is the movement toward creativity. It can be described as generosity. In movement, generosity, like compassion, can be seen through extension. The more generous I become, the more the life force can flow through me. The more I can express the things that touch me deeply in life, the more I am able to exchange energy with another.

Expression can be a willingness to open up my territory, and, with it, my compassion. As I open up and interact with other energies, creative manifestations are born out of the interactions. Art, music, and writing are the children of the interplay between my aliveness and the aliveness in the environment.

However, expression needs a balancing factor. The degree to which I open and extend is the degree in which I need a stable base. Overexpression leads to instability. If more energy comes through and out of me than I can ground, then I will begin to exhibit inappropriate behavior. Overexpression usually has a hysterical or aggressive quality about it. The antidote to this problem is containment.

In some cases, containment is appropriate. Listening to criticism is like being grabbed or punched. Both are incoming energy. Practicing dealing with incoming energy will result in my being able to tolerate the building up of energy inside myself. This capacity for containing energy can help me learn to tolerate even the difficult and unpleasant parts of myself. This is where compassion must start: with myself and with containment. It must be noted, though, that containing is different from repressing, blocking, or fighting energy within myself. When I repress, I tighten and resist; when I contain, I open, relax, and hold or make room for what is happening.

## THE CONNECTING THREAD: AWARENESS

We can refine and balance our energy through practice and discipline by focusing our attention in particular ways. Each person must find a way—a path of self-cultivation—to travel. The principles of aikido are not reserved for training on the mat: they can inform our whole lives. If we create a balanced environment, then we can watch how our energy begins to shape and organize itself. The ideal is an energy system that is flexible and can respond to situations spontaneously and appropriately. Our sense of time, space, and energy are all inter-related. When we focus on one, the others are affected.

The connecting thread is awareness. Awareness allows us to direct our attention, which affects our sense of time, space, and energy. When we become aware that we are speeding, we can apply our awareness and our training and slow ourselves down. Often we can accomplish more when we are not speeding and are more conscious of details. As we slow down, we can become aware of the space around us. When there is more space, time doesn't feel like such a pressure. As we become conscious that there is plenty of time and plenty of space, our energy begins to balance itself. When our energy is balanced, there is a feeling of more space. Each element affects the other, and our awareness is the glue of the situation.

This inquiry is a lifelong endeavor. Even if we should gain an important insight into one aspect of ourselves, there are still other, deeper layers of understanding and wisdom to be explored. As we explore time, space, and energy, we can feel the magnificence of our lives, the endless possibilities that are available to us. We have only to open our senses. Our appreciation of and openness to the potential for wise, compassionate action allow this type of action to manifest itself through us. And as we deepen and mature through these experiences, a quality of virtue begins to shine through our actions.

*chapter nine*

# UNDERSTANDING
# THE VERTICAL

*To discover that nothing is permanent is of tremendous*
*importance for only then is the mind free, then you can*
*look, and in that there is great joy.*

> —J. Krishnamurti, *Freedom from the Known*

## BETWEEN HEAVEN AND EARTH

A number of years ago, I sustained an injury to my right knee during an evening practice. I tore my anterior cruciate ligament and the cartilage inside my knee. For a year, I wore a brace made of stainless steel and fiberglass that had been fitted to my leg. Its design was such that I couldn't fold my leg underneath me in the normal *seiza*, or seated, position. I had to sit with my leg to one side in a way that torqued my right hip and ankle.

The approach that I had always taken in my training was to ground incoming energy by taking it downward, toward the mat. This approach was based on the premise that grounding it would neutralize it. I was often able to do this. But as my knee improved and I started practicing more intensely again, the combination of the torquing and my approach of redirecting incoming energy created pain and weakness in my right hip, knee, and ankle.

Throughout many years of practice, I had developed an ability to take pressure. I experienced myself as being strong under pressure. My right side, however, continued to be painful and weak. I changed to a lighter brace, which allowed me to fold my legs in a balanced way, but the pattern of discomfort remained. Neither Western nor holistic medicine could change or affect the condition. The situation began to change only when I started to find ways to "lighten up." In retrospect, I probably had many hints encouraging me in that direction, but it was so contrary to my thinking and my training that I ignored them.

During this time, I was investigating Native American practices. I participated in sweat lodge ceremonies, in which spirits of the four directions, north, south, east, and west, as well as spirits of above and below, heaven and Earth, are invited to hold, protect, and inform the process of the ceremony. At one point during one of these events, I received a strong impression that O'Sensei's spirit was trying to send me a message. Perhaps it was my inner wisdom disguised as O'Sensei. In any case, the message was that I was to consider myself "between heaven and Earth." The heaven part seemed to be emphasized.

At first it was difficult for me to really receive the message that heaven, or above, was a place of healing and power. I had always tried hard to be "grounded" and not "spacey." My understanding had been that down was where a person was strong, relaxed, and powerful, and up was where a person was lightweight, weak, and a space cadet. But the message was clear: I needed to cultivate the upward direction of my practice. One way to do this was to focus on balancing my energy field. I kept inquiring, *What it would be like if the energy above my head were equal to the energy below my feet, the feeling of the gravitational pull?* I made progress, but when I wasn't paying attention, I would slip back into my habit of over-weighing or loading my system. Little by little, however, I was able to focus more on the upward flow.

It was the increasing physical discomfort that inspired me to pay more attention to how incoming energy was organizing itself in my body. It was during a class with a friend, Paul Ciske, who was teaching about posture and body alignment, that I finally felt and understood the strength of the vertical flow. Paul has a wonderful way of helping people find a posture that is light, clear, and balanced. I discovered that when I was in proper skeletal alignment, a strong pressure exerted from above allowed me to feel light and strong. I experienced what they talk about in physics: for every action, there is an equal and opposite reaction. When another person would exert pressure, there would be an automatic upward flow of energy. As long as I didn't involve my muscles and simply allowed the skeleton to hold the pressure as it was designed to do, my system automatically balanced the pressure in an upward direction. All I had to do was enjoy it.

Gone was the feeling of "taking it," "loading up," or "handling" the pressure. Instead, the pressure was handling itself. It is important here to remember the principle, Energy follows attention. By concentrating on the downward direction all the time, I was unintentionally creating an energy imbalance. By allowing my energy to flow equally up and down, the energy could organize and balance itself. Prior to this realization, I had thought that the only alternative to taking the energy down was an option that I had tried to inhibit for years: the "right back at you" option, a reflex only too familiar to my reactive temperament. Allowing the energy to move up and down through me instead of down and into me was a liberating shift.

In receiving energy, it helps to think of the energy pattern as vertical rather than horizontal. From the horizontal viewpoint, the energy pattern tends to come into me or go right back at you. In the vertical way of receiving energy, there is plenty of room for the Earth and sky to absorb and organize the pressure. I now enjoy the sensation of lightening up under pressure. I tend to smile more, feel softer, and be able to accept the situation without feeling that I have to endure it.

## VERTICAL AND HORIZONTAL ENERGY FLOWS

The core of the body is primarily vertical in nature. From the cortex to the perineum, the lines of movement, from gross to subtle, flow in helixes within the verticality of the head, neck, and torso. From this established central column, energy moves out, expanding into the world of people and things. Equally, energy moves inward from the external world toward the central column. A person's response to incoming energy is usually a matter of conditioning. A person may either attempt to repel the incoming energy or absorb it by taking it into himself or herself. Or the person may do both. By studying himself or herself carefully, a person can observe his or her own responses to incoming energy. In most cases, the conditioned tendency is not the most efficient, compassionate way to handle this incoming energy.

We can use the principle from posture practice to deal with incoming energy. If we align ourselves between the natural gravitational pull and the dynamic upward response to it, then we can be in a situation of pressure without "loading up." We don't have to take the pressure: instead, we can allow it to move through us. As it comes into us, it is dispersed upward and downward equally. Through practice, we can recover long-forgotten pathways of energy flow. If we keep relating to the energy helixes, to the vertical flow of life moving through our systems, then we can receive intensity without it overwhelming or damaging us.

Energy itself is not a problem. Essentially, it is simply the vibration of the life force in our bodies. It is only when it meets resistance and is not able or allowed to organize itself that it can become difficult and dangerous. When this happens, the sense of coherence is diminished and the sense of anarchy is increased. When energy meets resistance, it increases rather than decreases. We think that by resisting pressure, we can make it stop or go away. This is an illusion. The more we resist, the stronger it gets. And so the dilemma arises: if we don't resist, then we will be overwhelmed, annihilated; if we do resist, then what we resist will become more powerful.

Looking at it in another way, the gravitational pull created by the Earth's core is balanced by the upward, vertical pull of the Earth's rotation. The Earth is spinning at a speed of 1,000 miles per hour. This creates a strong centrifugal force that would fling us into space were it not for gravity. By focusing our attention on both the centrifugal and gravitational forces, we can perceive that we are perfectly balanced between the two, that we can be grounded and light at the same time. This sense of balance creates a feeling of acceptance. We recognize that there is room for us, for whatever is happening; that there is no need to resist. What comes toward us can be directed up or down equally. It doesn't need to get stuck inside us or weigh us down.

William Johnston describes vertical and horizontal thinking from a similar perspective:

Vertical thinking is existential in that it does away with differences, distinctions, quiddities, and essences in order to find the unity of all things. This is mysticism. The second kind of thinking, which I have called horizontal, is found when the mind, preoccupied principally with the stream of consciousness passing before it, is taken up with diversity rather than unity—hence it stresses essences, quiddities, differences. Vertical or existential thinking concentrates on the fact *that* things are, seeing the unity of all being: horizontal or essential thinking concentrates on *what* things are, seeing their diversity.[1]

As in the ancient symbol of the cross, the vertical is established before the horizontal. In the world of nature, the plant establishes the vertical stalk and root before it spreads its branches. We must strengthen our relationship to ourselves first. This is the meaning of the vertical. We need to relate to our bodies, to the Earth, to our spirit or inspiration, and to our life force. Once this is established in a visceral, enthusiastic way, we become strong enough to relate skillfully with others, with the horizontal.

If I do not strengthen my connection with myself, then I become dependent on others for my sense of well-being. Who I am becomes what people think of me. I then begin to dominate or manipulate others in order to reassure myself of who I am. The question is, Who am I without other people? Do I have a healthy, happy relationship with myself? Am I aligned with my morality, compassion, and virtue? Without a good, strong vertical core, I will collapse into the horizontal, into a world of codependence and neediness or control in relationship to others. The result, when I depend on people for confirmation or happiness, is pain and suffering.

## BALANCING THE HORIZONTAL WITH THE VERTICAL

Much of the socialization process in our Western culture has to do with the acquisition of things and credentials that win approval from others. This emphasis on material goods and achievements draws us outward toward people and things, rather than inward toward that which relates to the spirit or the divine. We learn that manipulating people and controlling situations is the road to power and happiness.

It may take a personal crisis for us to turn inward, upward, or downward. Only when we realize that the world around us is unreliable do we seek elsewhere. At first, we usually don't really understand that the external world is unstable. We may think that we are not behaving properly, that it is our fault that everything is falling apart. Or we may decide that it is the other person who is the problem, that what we need is a new friend or partner. Perhaps we think that our parents are the problem: we may embark upon a lengthy therapeutic process to clarify the details of how our parents are the problem.

All of this functions on the horizontal plane: the situation is still about ourselves and others. We may even temporarily find an "other" who is stable, kind, and wise, and we may become attached to this person, thinking that he or she can make us happy. But even if this person is centered and balanced, he or she, too, is inexorably bound by the laws of time and subject to disease and death. This person may leave us—abandon us—through illness or death. If this person has become our center, our raison d'être, and he or she falls ill or dies, we may once again feel betrayed and feel that the world has lost its cohering principle.

Everything in the physical world is subject to change. Nothing is completely stable. Yet we keep searching in the physical world for a stable reference point. We have been socialized to relate in this way to the world. Because our sense of our own moral compass has not been activated, we use the etiquette of accepted social behavior to stabilize ourselves. But in the end, this will not satisfy our spiritual yearning. Our true path is one of self-development and growth.

As William Johnston writes,

Growth, then, demands detachment; and both growth and detachment are difficult for man. Psychologists who think like Fromm will say that it is precisely the refusal to accept the fact of growth that causes complexes, psychological retardations, and neuroses. For human nature shrinks from growth just as the child is reluctant to leave its mother's womb and its mother's breast, and as the adolescent shrinks from the unknown adult world that rises before him. For psychological growth is a journey into unknown territory; and no one likes to leave the drab Platonic cave where he sits in sad security. Hence, man must muster all his psychological force to overcome each crisis and to avoid slipping back into infantilism.[2]

It is not always easy to keep growing. If we are to "master [our] psychological force," then we need some motivation to do so. Somehow we must find a way to stop looking to the physical world of people and things for our sense of stability and well-being. We need to look inward, upward, and downward. We need to relate to our lives in the moment, to become aware of the presence of the earth below us, and the air, the sky, and the breeze around us, and to the sensation of life pulsing through us. Again and again, we have to return to ourselves until our sense of ourselves and the present moment is as strong as the pull toward or against people and things. When there is balance between these two energies, then we can begin the task of relating skillfully to the world around us.

In fact, when we are more calm and balanced, our sense of ourselves, which is primarily vertical in its ability to be still and present in the moment, is clear enough that it can inform us about how to interact with the world of people and things: the horizontal. This is allowing the intuition, our inner wisdom, to form the basis of our ethical and moral behavior. Our sense of autonomy allows us to grow and mature from a stable core so that we can respond to the events in our lives with dignity and presence. The energy of the world of people and things then helps us to continue to cultivate or clarify our relationship with ourselves, our feeling for our spiritual purpose, our compassion, and our connection to the divine. Then when we observe suffering or beauty, we have a context: we have cultivated the depth and the space in which to work with the experience.

So how do we strengthen our sense of ourselves, the vertical quality of our lives? It is through our willingness to continue a disciplined practice with open hearts. The principles of aikido are helpful and always available if we are willing to incorporate them into our everyday existence. We must cultivate the center if we want to be centered. To be virtuous, we must cultivate that which leads to virtue.

## CULTIVATING OUR VERTICAL CORE

I have been fascinated by the symbolic relationship between heaven and Earth for a long time. There is a heaven and Earth aikido technique that involves leading the incoming energy from the partner in both directions simultaneously. Native American spiritual practices emphasize heaven and Earth as the father and mother aspects of the universe. I have had luminous moments in which I have felt myself held lovingly between the forces of heaven and Earth and invited to be a living, dynamic bridge between the two, the human embodiment and a child of the masculine and feminine elements from above and below.

When I am balanced, energy flows up through my body and then out toward the world of relationships. Life grows up, but in order to sustain itself, it must be stabilized in the Earth. If I lose my balance and become overinvolved with a person or task, then the sustaining power that comes from the vertical flow of heaven and Earth diminishes and my world begins to narrow. If I can relate to the strength in my core, then I can keep a connection with a larger view of life while interacting with the person or task before me.

The vertical is our relationship to our archetypal, or original, selves. It represents basic goodness, uprightness, and the divine aspect of life itself. It is the basis for our moral behavior and our compassion. It is the reference point from which we draw the line as to the limits of what we will and will not do while creating minimal harm. Traditionally, religions have represented this area of our lives. However, in some cases, the religious structure is too limited or rigid. Many of us don't want to be threatened by negative consequences as a motivation to become more respectable or agreeable participants of society. Religious etiquette is not enough.

However, the principles of kindness, respect, and generosity continue to be timeless motivators in drawing an ethical line. The key to cultivating these principles is to bring our attention to them again and again. A religious service, once a week, is not enough to balance six days of resentment and desire. Daily discipline builds and strengthens a strong vertical core of integrity.

Attentional practices that involve visual, auditory, and sensate concentration can help us uncover the natural strength in the core. In some traditions, a physical representation of love, such as Christ or the Buddha, is visualized inside the body at the core of a person's being, emanating love and light through the physical body. Prayers are an auditory manifestation of positive energy flowing through the body. Sensate practices focus on qualities of warmth, aliveness, lightness, or heaviness that cultivate a positive inner feeling. These practices are repeated again and again so that a specific, clear sense of strength in the core begins to emerge.

This sense of strength is not a vague sense of "okayness." Numbness can be mistaken for feeling okay. We may think that if it something doesn't feel bad, then it must be all right. Upon closer investigation, however, we might find that there is no feeling at all. This is not what is meant by cultivating a positive core. A positive core has a strong clarity of presence and confidence. When the core is strong enough that it has a feeling of constancy and reliability, virtue is emerging. It is this core that is able to function when negative or threatening energy arises. It has a reference point and a vitality.

How deep and reliable is our connection to this vertical core? Can the connection withstand aggression? Is the connection equal to that of the Dalai Lama or Mother Teresa? When the Buddha sat under the bodhi tree and was tempted with all that the world had to offer— wealth, physical love, and power—his core was equal to the horizontal pull. Christ also was tempted and chose the vertical. What is important to remember is that they did it without regret, without feeling conflicted. Their virtue was able to withstand the pressure of temptation.

When our shadow side—our fears, desires, and insecurities— emerges, we can do our best to accept and acknowledge it, and we can choose to relate to our positive core. We don't have to reject the one: it is more a matter of choosing the other. To this end, I use the "Yes, and" technique: I acknowledge a negative thought or feeling and then shift my attention to a positive, more spacious thought form. If self-criticism arises, then I might say to myself, *Yes, that was stupid,* and *what is it like to feel more softness inside me?*

In this way, I strengthen my ability to relate with the vertical and not let myself dwell in the horizontal. It is not a matter of ignoring the negative. I have a genuine respect for this part of my psyche: hence, my "Yes." The discipline that I am cultivating is a commitment to develop my core so it can someday equal the strength of the shadow. The shadow is our motivator. We feel its negative effects and we want to be free from the neediness and aggression it creates in us. The vertical, the positive, has to be a viable choice. If there is no substance to it, then obviously, the shadow can dominate. If the shadow becomes dominant, then we can at least recognize and respect its strength. We can acknowledge that this is where we are: this is our starting place. We will have to work for freedom from our own neediness and aggression. Discipline is the key. Discipline cultivates an ability to see deeply, to see things as they are, not just as they appear on the surface.

The vertical must be as strong, if not stronger, than the horizontal. Our love for goodness must be stronger than our desire for things and for approval. Virtue not only knows the direction of our moral compass, it is drawn unhesitatingly in that direction. Virtue is the result of a deep motivation that springs from a natural desire for harmony, for the vertical connection to the divine, and for the luminous presence in all of us. Virtue does not come from a motivation based on image and an approval from others, that is, the horizontal.

It is possible to see integrity and virtue in the way people carry themselves. Aikido encourages good posture. My teachers are always reminding me to stand up straight, and, as a teacher, I remind my students to be attentive to their posture. An upright and relaxed posture has an elegance that is pleasing to the eye. Good posture projects the energy of the vertical. It is from this vertical core that we can radiate our energy out into the world. Our responses then are not a matter of trying to control others: rather, they are an attempt to connect and communicate from our core. It is a pleasure for others to feel the positive flow of energy that is emanating from our strong center.

## LEVELS OF EXCELLENCE

What is the secret of these people who excel? Whether the excellence is of the mind, of the body, or of the heart, some people seem to be free of the constrictions of time, space, or energy that limit most of us to what we define as normal functioning. They do the extraordinary with what seems like a natural ease. Albert Einstein's mental prowess, Morihei Ueshiba's physical abilities, and Mother Teresa's loving heart are the exception rather than the rule. Yet those people who are able to tap into a kind of freedom from limitation say that there is nothing extraordinary about what they do, that others with an equal level of commitment could do the same. They say that it is easy.

What is it that allows these people to be free from the stress that we experience in approaching the same tasks? Some basic principles can enhance our ability to fulfill more of our potential. Commitment, focus, and repetition are the building blocks of excellence. But without inspiration or a deep desire to go beyond our perceived limitations, we will only develop good—but not extraordinary—abilities. So how can we become inspired to the point of willingly changing our lives? What is it that draws us to discipline rather than ease? How can we willingly give up the latter for the former and allow the virtue of unconditional love to become the fruit of our commitment to discipline?

Eastern psychology talks about elements such as karma, luck, and auspicious timing. We in the West view the extraordinary as arising from free will or genetics. The underlying principle of each of these ideas is that there is something larger that we draw from, be it a spiritual force or our genetic pool. Jung's collective unconscious and the Eastern notion of karma are different ways of saying that we are more than our physical bodies or our cognitive minds. These views hold that life is light, energy, and vibration. Perhaps our feelings of limitation may be self-imposed. Perhaps inspiration comes from a belief in our limitless potential.

Consciousness of this kind is able to relate to a state of being that lies beyond the mind, that resonates with the entire universe, and knows that the universe is interconnected rather than separate elements. If there is complete confidence in the interconnection of all things, then there is no sense of having to do something to something else. Instead, there is a doing with, there is a joining, so that *the situation works in collaboration with itself.*

The fact that the situation works in collaboration with itself may account for the humility that is usually found in people with extraordinary abilities. If everything works together to produce a result, then why should anyone take credit for an accomplishment? What may seem like an amazing accomplishment to us is, for them, simply part of the ongoing flow of the universe. We can make the choice: we can relate to the perspective of unity or the perspective of separation. By relating to unity and seeing ourselves as part of the whole of creation, we can draw on the energy of the universe.

The battle between unity and separation is ancient. We all seek the resolution of our inner conflicts. If leaders such as O'Sensei and Gandhi are our models, then we can see the benefits of unity. Their achievement was the result of their commitment. And their examples can encourage us to commit ourselves to finding our own ways of living lives of integrity and unconditional love.

春風以接人
秋霜以自肅

*part three*

FRUITION

*chapter ten*

# FREEDOM

*The truth is we are not yet free; we have merely achieved the freedom*
*to be free, the right not to be oppressed.*

—Nelson Mandela, *Long Walk to Freedom*

## DIFFERING VIEWS OF FREEDOM

I became motivated to write this book when I was working with women in prison. I had been teaching the practices of aikido-based conflict resolution, meditation, and yoga for about three years when I began to see some real changes in attitude and behavior in some of the women. I sensed that where there once had been resentment or manipulation, there was now an emerging etiquette, morality, and compassion. Some of the women in the program were becoming freer than some people I knew who were not in prison. The notion of freedom began to fascinate me, and has led me to examine my own beliefs and inquire into other points of view on the subject.

When the question What is freedom? is posed, what is the first thought that pops into our minds? Children tend to respond that freedom is the ability to do certain things: come and go when and where they please, eat what they please, say what they please, and so on. Many adults remark that freedom means to be free from emotional hang-ups, such as anger, jealousy, longing, and confusion. Like children, politicians and people who are incarcerated tend to say that freedom means that they can go where they want when they want, say what they want—and make as much money as they want.

The aikido mat is a laboratory that allows me to study what happens to my personal sense of freedom when I am being attacked. I am always amazed at how primal my response is when I am grabbed or struck at with considerable speed and power. Even after many years of training, I often feel my body tense and contract when I am attacked with intensity.

Practice and repetition have taught me to correct this; that is, to recover a more relaxed and expansive state. The speed with which I can recover from tension is the key to maintaining a fluid response to such an attack. If I can remain relaxed or recover within a second, then I usually can bring a sense of freedom to the situation. This is because when I am able to feel relaxed and fluid, there seems to be plenty of time and options in a period that lasts about one to five seconds. I am able to do this when I relate to my partner as being an extension of me, rather than a separate entity attacking me. I am then free from having to defend myself. I am free to move within the dynamic of our relationship.

Of course, what happens on the mat is a metaphor for any moment in the rest of my life. A tense phone call or a driver honking at me or a memory of a rude remark can all make me feel attacked. From the aikido perspective, these experiences are opportunities to relax, expand, and feel the fluidity of the moment. Aikido encourages me to be soft, strong, and flexible, even in difficult circumstances.

The Buddhist view of freedom is liberation from the continuing cycle of birth and death. Like in the movie *Groundhog Day*, in which the hero is forced to relive the same day again and again, we must keep being reborn until we get it right. Liberation comes when there is nothing more to get right.

A further step beyond liberation is the concept of *bodhisattva*. To take the *bodhisattva* path, we make a vow that even if everything is finished and there is nothing more to do on a personal level, we will continue to be reborn to help others until everyone is liberated from the wheel of birth and death. This freedom is not only an individual thing but also a collective approach.

Peace Pilgrim has this to say on the subject of freedom:

> No one is truly free who is still attached to material things, or to places, or to people. We must be able to use things when we need them and then relinquish them without regret when they have outlived their usefulness. We must be able to appreciate and enjoy the places where we tarry, and yet pass on without anguish when we are called elsewhere. We must be able to live in loving association with people without feeling that we possess them and must run their lives. Anything that you strive to hold captive will hold you captive, and if you desire freedom you must give freedom.[1]

Clearly, there are many perspectives on the issue of freedom. The idea of freedom also implies its opposite: incarceration, subjection. This was my starting place: questioning our experience of freedom. In my research, certain themes stood out. They are, in some ways, at the heart of the path of self-development. These themes are freedom as discipline, freedom as space, and freedom as responsibility.

## FREEDOM AS DISCIPLINE

"The founders of the classical budo systems," says Donn F. Draeger, "prescribed certain disciplines to open the mind's eye. These disciplines are akin to pure introspective mysticism; one can only enter mystic experience through direct participation."[2]

We tend to be creatures of habit. Our habits solidify around pleasure and pain, desire and distaste. It is through the discipline of practicing alternative responses that we develop the possibility of having a number of ways to relate to a given situation. In aikido, I discovered that my tendency to want to get control of my partner when I felt threatened precluded getting control of myself. I worked on this by withdrawing my attention from my partner, placing it within myself, and focusing on developing different options or ways of moving in my own body. That way, my partner is drawn into my movement instead of me being drawn into his or her movement during the attack.

The tendency to contract during an encounter is another powerful habit that I have found can be countered through disciplined practice. The antidote to contraction is, of course, expansion. Again and again, hundreds and thousands of times, I have had to repeat the exercise of opening and expanding my body, my energy, and my mind, so that the possibility of extension as generosity could be encoded in my nervous system, generosity being the emotional quality that I associate with extension and expansion.

Discipline can allow us to have a quality such as generosity as a possible response to a situation that feels aggressive or threatening. Each time that I train, I encourage myself toward this expansiveness, this generosity. Instead of indulging my urge to "get" my partner, I work with the feeling of giving to my partner. Through the discipline of repetition, this awareness is beginning to become a genuine possibility in my life, which, in turn, inspires my practice in aikido.

It is not easy to cultivate an attitude that is about expanding the ability to give and be generous. The emphasis in today's society is on protecting the self and accumulating more. In order to be generous, we must develop a mature perspective in which we can see that we are individuals and, at the same time, intrinsically connected to one another, and that both of these aspects of the human condition need attention. This requires the discipline of self-awareness, of separating our wants from our needs. If we can learn to develop the discipline of self-control, then we can strengthen our confidence in ourselves as strong, loving individuals. We would then be able to embody Nelson Mandela's vision to "live in a way that respects and enhances the freedom of others."[3]

It takes discipline to stay on the path of self-cultivation, for our culture emphasizes self-defense, self-forgetting, and selfishness. Through practice, we can strengthen our confidence in our sense of ourselves as individuals who are also connected to the universe in a loving way. As Swami Rudrananda writes, "It is the most difficult of all searchings for we are afraid to stand alone and be free. For countless centuries man has been a dependent animal. It is not necessary to separate us from our society but for us to function independently."[4]

If we can focus our minds in the way that we wish, then we will be able to see different possibilities in a situation. If we are not swayed by our wants, then we will have more freedom to choose an option. Discipline gives us flexibility. Instead of always acting or reacting in the same way, we can respond to the possibilities. This opens the door to creativity. Because we are not limited to our fight or flight response, because we have trained ourselves to relax and be more open, we can allow our intuitive, creative forces to respond to the situation. Discipline gives us stability. It gives us the ability to be patient, which allows us to wait and look at the more panoramic view. We can see things as they are without so much of our personal bias getting in the way.

One of my teachers, Chögyam Trungpa Rinpoche, a Tibetan Buddhist and author of *Shambhala: The Sacred Path of the Warrior,* made a distinction between taming the mind and training the mind. In the first level, I must tame my attention. This is the most basic level of discipline. It's like training a dog. Before I can teach a dog to do tricks, the dog must be able to respond to some basic commands, such as "Heel." Similarly, the basic discipline of taming my attention is to teach it to come back and focus wherever I direct it: to "heel." Once I have tamed my attention, then I can begin to refine my attention. This is a deeper level of discipline.

I attended a lecture given by another Tibetan Buddhist teacher who compared the mind to an elephant. He told us that in India, where he lives, there are many elephants. He said that a well-trained elephant is of great use: a great deal can be accomplished with its strength and power. But an untrained elephant is very destructive. I was particularly taken by this image, because, at times, my mind feels like an untrained elephant: large and clumsy. It was inspiring to recognize that I could put that power to use in a constructive way.

Discipline helps us to begin to organize our energy. It keeps us from losing our way. It is a tool to help us work with the stuff of life, to shape it and refine it, to uncover the compassion, the virtue, and the freedom that is inherently ours. Lao Tzu says it beautifully:

> Understand this if nothing else: spiritual freedom
>    and oneness with the Tao are not randomly
>    bestowed gifts, but the rewards of conscious
>    self-transformation and self-evolution."[5]

## FREEDOM AS SPACE

Hiroshi Ikeda Sensei says, "Freedom is space."[6] And J. Krishnamurti writes, "If you are too close, you see only the various separate branches. So to see the whole of anything there must be—not the space that the word creates—but the space of freedom. Only in freedom can you see the whole."[7]

The black belt test in aikido has a requirement called *randori*, in which a person is attacked by two or more people. The candidates are encouraged to practice this exercise as part of the preparation for their test. Sometimes at the end of class, I will call a candidate out to the center of the mat and ask for two or three volunteer attackers. I have noticed that if the person who is being attacked can relax and move toward the spaces in the room instead of toward the people, an interesting phenomenon takes place. The attackers begin to become less focused and, at times, seem to collide with or confuse one another. If the person being attacked focuses solely on the attackers, then the attackers become focused on the person. When there are a number of attackers who are fast and strong, the situation can begin to feel tight and claustrophobic, and often the person who is being attacked gets caught or struck.

However, if the person's focus is on the spaces in between and at the back of the attackers instead of their bodies, then the feeling tone of the event changes completely. The person being attacked appears to be moving more slowly and easily than the attackers, and the attackers seem to be less focused on the person and more involved with one another and the spacing of their bodies. This spacing is like intervals in a musical score. The intervals allow the musical notes to be suspended in order to convey a particular feeling or intensity. Without the intervals, all the notes would be pushed together, creating a tight wall of sound. The intervals open them up, allowing us to appreciate the nuances of the music.

This reminds me of photography. There is a big difference between art photography and the family photo style of photography. In the family photo style, the focus is usually on the group, that is, getting all the bodies or things into the photo. In art photography, the space, shape, and texture around the person or thing is as important as the person or thing. In the same vein, I encourage students to do the *randori* practice artistically, making the space as important as the people. This is easier said than done, for when someone is threatening or exciting, he or she is compelling, and it is difficult not to focus on the person creating the threat or the excitement.

One key to my being able to take my attention off the attackers and put it on the space—that is, the area around the attackers—is to make the space itself attractive. If I have an interest in the shape and the texture of the space, then it is easier to move in that direction. It takes concentration and discipline to see and feel the space and be able to move into it while inviting the attackers into that spacious quality as well. This exercise is intense: it requires a lot of practice and a willingness to explore relating with space in an artistic fashion while feeling pressured.

This practice is, once again a metaphor for any aspect of our lives in which a number of things seem to be coming at us. The practice could represent a busy schedule, a family get-together, or our minds when we sit quietly with the intention of calming ourselves. Cultivating a sense of space offers us feelings of freedom and flexibility, and a larger perspective on the situation.

Space is usually thought of as an expanse or an empty area. Containment is about being able to hold, to have a capacity for, something. Life offers us an abundant quantity of energy and aliveness. How we handle this endowment has much to do with our experience of life as satisfying or unsatisfying. Our bodies and our energy fields are the containers that hold the potential of space and energy—the amount of aliveness usually perceived as spirit or presence—in our lives. If someone has a strong spirit and a powerful presence, that person is able to contain and tolerate a great deal of energy within his or her system. So how is it that this occurs?

One important factor is the ability to relax and open all the channels so that there is more room and the flow of energy entering us is not impeded. This means that the breath, the blood flow, and the energy along the spine are not constricted in any way. When we tighten up, we constrict the flow of aliveness. A sense of containment means that we can tolerate sensations of energy and intense emotions until they have matured and self-organized into information and creative action. We can tolerate them because we have made space for them. It is like recycling: instead of throwing things away—the equivalent of "freaking out" emotionally—we can work with and hold feelings until we have a better understanding of the information they contain. These emotions are, in essence, pure energy. If we don't reject their intensity, then they can be refined into compassion and creativity.

Our ability to turn stress and pressure into compassion and productivity is the result of the fact that we cultivate and maintain space in our minds, our thought processes, so that our awareness can move freely without getting hung up on a fear or a desire. A sense of spaciousness gives us the freedom to walk in the world knowing that whatever we encounter will become part of the creative process. It is possible to discover that fear, sadness, and frustration, if they are held without tension and allowed to self-organize, will become understanding, compassion, and creativity.

Space is intrinsic to the quest for freedom, and how it is understood, formed, and used depends on the container. Verse 11 from the Tao Te Ching is a delightful description of this relationship, and of how important respect for both the container and the space is if a person is to function skillfully in a situation:

Thirty spokes will converge
In the hub of a wheel;
But the use of the cart
Will depend on the part
Of the hub that is void.

With a wall all around
A clay bowl is molded;
But the use of the bowl
Will depend on the part
Of the bowl that is void.

Cut out windows and doors
In the house as you build;
But the use of the house
Will depend on the space
In the walls that is void.

So advantage is had
From whatever is there;
But usefulness rises
From whatever is not.[8]

Freedom can be the experience of space within the container of our lived experience. When our minds, hearts, and psyches are spacious, there is room to function. Functioning out of the space of stillness is a virtue of freedom: it is a creative act.

I have a friend, Nicola Geiger, whose being is filled with love, laughter, and space. A visit with her helps me to remember how contented I feel when I relax, laugh, and allow myself the space to be, to listen, and to see. Not long ago she made this comment:

I am now seventy-eight, and the other night, I was asked the question, "Do you still feel useful?" I feel that I am as useful as I have always been. True, I can't do certain things any longer. That's fine. As one ages, one has to learn to gracefully surrender to one's body. But that has nothing to do with my total, inner focus and readiness and just being. To be able to listen and to do whatever I can do. And not to judge at all or compare this and that. We are so imprisoned by what other people think. There is no freedom in that sense. The most wonderful thing is to laugh at myself. Each moment of time is a totality. I feel that so strongly.[9]

Nicola taught me an important lesson with regard to judgment. Comparing and judging take up a tremendous amount of room in my being. When I am involved in that kind of mental experience, there is no room for appreciation. When I can suspend criticism and judgment, there is all the room I need in order to see and be.

Space is always there. We are free to relate with it. It is a matter of where we focus our attention. Certainly, there are people and events that are powerful forces in our lives, but we can cultivate the strength not to be obsessed with them. We can acknowledge them, relate with them, and cultivate a habit of appreciation and wonder. When we realize that it is possible to do this, we may feel a response within us that could be considered responsibility.

## FREEDOM AS RESPONSIBILITY

Hiroshi Ikeda Sensei says, "Responsibility is common sense. In life you have to have common sense."[10] And Nelson Mandela writes, "for with freedom come responsibilities."[11]

When I was in South Africa, I watched a TV show in which a panel of blacks was discussing the challenges of bringing South Africa into social balance. Apartheid had been abolished and the people of color were "free," so South Africans had to find a way to handle this freedom. A comment by one panelist impressed me. He said, "Freedom is not free. It is a responsibility: it takes effort and sacrifice. There must be cooperation, initiative, and a cause."

From one point of view, freedom and responsibility are intertwined. If space is one of the essential aspects of freedom, then, because we all live in community, we must understand the issue of everyone's need for space. A person's responsibility begins with respect for the self, for his or her own individuality. If a person is aware of his or her own need for respect and space, then it will only makes sense to give the same kind of respect and space to others. In order for a person to fulfill himself or herself as an individual and as member of the community, he or she must be willing to take the responsibility to encourage respect for each individual's need for space. From the point of view of community, the two—self and other—can't be separated: what one person does affects other people.

While in South Africa, I met an older woman named June Jones, who ran a spiritual practices center. Jones radiated happiness and light. When I asked her about her thoughts on freedom and its relationship to responsibility, she said, "Freedom is responsibility. This is not a problem: it is a natural outcome of community." [12] I was struck by her comment, because it implies that responsibility is natural, a normal part of who we are, rather than something that is learned or imposed by an external authority, be it God, a teacher, or a political authority. How, then, can we uncover that natural sense of responsibility, so that our behavior genuinely reflects freedom and responsibility?

We are all interrelated. Awareness of this creates a responsibility. We have a responsibility and an ability to respond to our environment and to the people around us. In Buddhism, the *mahayana* path is sometimes referred to as the greater vehicle, because it is seen as the wide highway of compassionate action. It is this *mahayana* principle, the principle of expansiveness, that seeks to include all people in the quest for freedom. Our willingness to cultivate our process of self-development has within it a centrifugal force, an innate tendency to expand and include others in our vision of freedom. Through self-development, education, and understanding, we can take the responsibility to move from our tendencies toward self-absorption, chaos, and anarchy to moral responsibility, compassion, and virtue—and, ultimately, to freedom.

Without responsibility, our freedom remains the freedom of a child: it is merely freedom from constraints. We want to be free only for our own pleasure. This level of freedom is limited indeed. It needs to be contained by stringent etiquette, which in itself diminishes our experience of creativity and satisfaction. Without containment, the desire for pleasure can cause great pain and suffering because, when there is no consideration of the consequences of selfish behavior, there is no understanding of the results of such behavior. True freedom is the freedom to do something. Whether that doing is being still or being actively engaged in a task, we are participating consciously and willingly.

Once we can function independently, relax, and have confidence in who we are, we are able to handle the responsibility of teamwork and taking part in community. It's like the body: each part must be able to work individually and also in harmony with the other body parts. For instance, each arm and each leg has to be able to move independently. But for the whole body to move through space, both arms and legs need to work with the other body parts. Saotome Sensei explains this idea:

Training helps you to understand the physical function of each part: the hand, the foot, the *hara,* the center, the vision, the eyes—all kind of things. On the other side, you must learn your physical limitations. I cannot carry 300 pounds with one hand, so I understand the limitation in my body. For example, the hand has a limited function. So how do I support my hand? With my foot and other parts of the body. It is this kind of unification, this harmonious relationship, that leads to freedom. My right hand is limited, so I support it with the left. All parts of the body have a limited function, so my body must function in a kind of team-work. Then there is more freedom.

Social behavior is the same thing. You understand that your behavior is limited, so that makes you freer from injuries or accidents. If you are driving, you must respect the law. Then you are free to go where you please. The law is important because it provides security. Without the security of the law, it would be very dangerous to drive. But if you obey the law, you don't injure yourself and you don't injure others. Then we are free to drive where we want.

This is the kind of thing that education can teach. In a free, democratic society, the most important thing is education. On the spiritual side, education is essential, and the teaching of limitation with respect to freedom. We are not, for example, free to kill or to steal. We must respect other people's lives and their right to freedom.[13]

Understanding our limitations gives us respect for these limitations and a clear reference point from which to begin our work. Morality and compassion are the outcome of working skillfully with our limitations. We agree to take responsibility for ourselves, to work with what we have without complaining; we take the responsibility to become free. As Nelson Mandela points out at the beginning of this chapter, we are not yet free: we merely have the freedom to be free.

Our work is before us, and we have the freedom to do it, provided we are inspired and the committed.

My friend Nicola Geiger has found that inspiration and has made that commitment. She says, "I need to be responsible not to create suffering for others or for myself. That is the freedom that I have. And for that I'm immensely grateful, that I can be, just be, without judging whether I can or whether I can't."[14] She reports that this marvelous attitude is the result of committed practice. She has been meditating for more than sixty-five years and encourages others to begin right away with her favorite meditation: laughing meditation. She believes is that the system of a person who practices laughing meditation begins to resonate with laughing energy. As this laughing energy becomes familiar, the body becomes more open and tensions dissolve.

This quality of contagious delight is also an attribute of His Holiness the Dalai Lama's. He, too, advocates that a person take responsibility for reducing his or her own suffering and that of others. He says this: "The practice of these teachings . . . offer[s] the means to free oneself from delusion—a path that eventually leads to freedom from all suffering. . ."[15]

*chapter eleven*

# THE WAY: SELF-CULTIVATION

*The path to joy lies not in depending on external conditions, but in
undoing the conditioning of pleasure and pain which excites the mind
to search for satisfaction in the world outside.*

—Eknath Easwaran, *The Dhammapada*

## HAPPINESS

Self-cultivation gives a person the possibility of being able to expand
his or her capacity for open and loving behavior under all conditions,
including stress and conflict. It is the process of refining the awareness
of life in the present moment. The universe is a generous benefactor,
and the strength of a person's spirit enables him or her to receive its
gift. Happiness and the capacity for service and love are manifestations of the universal generosity available to everyone.

To me, one of the most destructive phrases in the English language
is "And they lived happily ever after." As a child, I wanted to believe
that, like Cinderella and like Snow White, my Prince Charming was
out there somewhere, and when we met, he would end all the pain and
loneliness in my life. Eventually, I realized that this was impossible,
and that not only did love relationships not make me happy, they
made me positively unhappy! I felt betrayed and resentful when I realized that I had been led to believe that I could be rescued by another.
Nevertheless, this myth had been implanted so deeply in my psyche
that it took a long time before I understood the truth that happiness

comes not from finding "Mr. Right" but from finding my Self.

Years ago, my daughter, Tiphani, articulated the same thing as we were driving to the coast. She said, "I realize that I have been looking for the right man who will make me feel like I am 'together.' I see now that I have to get myself together first, and then I can connect with someone who is more on that level." It is sad that children are led to believe that someone outside themselves will bring them happiness. When I work with people individually, I see great suffering generated by this myth. I wish that fairy tales ended with a phrase, "And they supported each other through the ups and downs of their lives with respect and with compassion."

The U.S. Declaration of Independence states that a person has the right to life, liberty, and the pursuit of happiness. How does an individual pursue happiness? Is it by getting or by giving? Does freedom imply happiness and happiness imply freedom? If a person becomes free from negative feelings, is he or she then free to be happy? How does a person's relationships and environment affect his or her sense of freedom and happiness? Perhaps happiness, like wisdom, is always present for an individual to discover. Just as the potential for a mature human being is contained in an embryo, so the potential for freedom and happiness is contained within every moment of a person's life.

Because aikido is noncompetitive in the sense that there is no official winner or loser, joy can be experienced while practicing. I have felt moments of great happiness in both the role of the *uke*, the attacker, and the *nage*, the one who throws. There is the joy of giving my body, of feeling my energy accepted and redirected, and of carving energy patterns through the air on my way to the mat. Learning to give and take energy skillfully so that no harm comes to either person takes time and careful development.

I am grateful for the environment of the dojo, where aikido and its principles can be practiced. The dojo is a laboratory where I can uncover what stands in the way of my happiness and discover ways to free myself from these hindrances. If a technique doesn't flow easily, then I can see my tendency to criticize myself or my partner. The same thing happens in my interactions with others off the mat. I now know that most of my difficulties are a result of my own resistance. When I can release my resistance, flow is restored to the situation.

Happiness is sometimes experienced as a sudden awakening, and sometimes it involves stages of growth. There is a Zen saying on the subject: "Before enlightenment, chop wood and carry water; after enlightenment, chop wood and carry water." This implies that moments of happiness are best supported by remembering to return to the present. We can connect with our inner core, whether things are difficult or whether they are easy. When our inner core strengthens and becomes a place of stillness, the door to divine love opens and moments of difficulty do not have to make us unhappy. Instead of being frustrated because our lives are not proceeding smoothly, we can appreciate the textures and stages that arise naturally in life.

## OUR INNER TERRAIN

It may be helpful to a person's attainment of happiness to have a kind of map that provides an aerial view of internal terrain, that allows a person to identify his or her location. It is my hope that this book will be such a map. An individual can locate himself or herself by recognizing the moments of anarchy, etiquette, morality, compassion, and virtue that are woven into the fabric of his or her life. A person's life is a tapestry of insights, feelings; the tapestry includes threads of the present moment and threads of all that has gone on before. The person is free to accept the richness of what he or she is or to resent the pattern and wish his or her life otherwise; the person is actually free to make the choice. Will that choice lead to happiness and freedom or frustration and unhappiness?

We are born from a state of connection (the Way). As we grow, we come to resist external control, which can mean that we are resistant and rebellious (anarchy). We then discover that there are rules that organize the separate pieces of life into accepted behavior (etiquette). The rules begin to take on meaning and give us a sense of purpose or direction (morality). We then realize that we are connected to others and develop a feeling of concern for their happiness or well-being (compassion). Next, we sense the need to find meaning in our lives and wish to make a contribution to life on this planet (virtue). We then surrender an individual identity, the ego, to the truth that we are all a part of life, that we are not separate, that one is all and all are one (the Way).

These stages do not always occur in this order. Overall development tends to follow this outline, but, in my daily awareness practice, I can suddenly find myself in a thought that I identify as anarchy, and then, if I can accept it and not struggle with the idea or feeling, it may switch to a sense of compassion.

## DIFFICULTIES AS OPPORTUNITIES

Aikido and awareness practice allow me to see the levels where my attention spends the most time. Often, simply by recognizing where my attention is and expanding myself to accept the truth that I am thinking such a thought, I begin a recycling process. The energy arising from the thought becomes a fuel that energizes my commitment to cultivating a more virtuous life, which leads to the Way of happiness and freedom. My commitment to practice must be revitalized constantly. Whatever comes up in myself can be recycled toward this end.

Our feelings of unhappiness and discontent are of our own making. We have the ability to end our suffering. If we can learn to view difficulties as opportunities, then whatever appears in our lives is useful. Instead of harshly judging or rejecting our thoughts and feelings, we can recycle them. Our difficult thoughts and feelings contain plenty of fuel, which keeps us from feeling depleted. Just as the plants by the side of the road use carbon monoxide for their growth, so, too, can we use the energy of our conflicts to move us along.

Each situation that arises is an opportunity to practice these abilities. Often we ignore these opportunities. Our minds jump to the future or the past. The details of the present are hazy and thus we miss the benefit yielded by the practice of working with what is in front of us. Self-cultivation is not always glamorous, and we don't always make obvious progress continuously. Sometimes we encounter periods where there seems to be no growth in our strengths or skills. My friend and aikido teacher George Leonard calls this a plateau. Authentic self-cultivation consists of a commitment strong enough to move us through a plateau.

## ACCEPTING WHO WE ARE

Usually, when we search for happiness and freedom, we come up against our limitations. We discover what appears to keep us from what we want. Most often, what we think will make us happy is found outside of ourselves. Desires for the perfect companion, the perfect job, the perfect house, or the perfect body create a feeling of separation. We are separate from our vision of happiness. The more we judge and compare, the more unhappy and stuck we feel.

O'Sensei says, "Winning means winning over the mind of discord in yourself."[1] So how is this achieved? It is through self-cultivation, through systematic practice, that a person can discover his or her own individual process that will lead that person to the Way. Principles of the kind are found in aikido and their accompanying exercises that strengthen physical, emotional, and spiritual vitality can give a person the self-confidence that opens the door to happiness. Self-confidence and happiness beget vitality, which gives a person the inspiration to continue to open his or her heart and mind. It is through understanding and accepting who he or she is that a person will experience the limitless joy of life.

The universe is not stingy. It is not withholding energy from us. It is we who tighten up in the face of life, we who are not allowing the energy to flow through us. It could be because we have forgotten that we are intrinsically connected to all things and believe that we are separate, are alone, and must protect ourselves.

Matter is made up of particles, cells, and a great deal of space. Every bit of space, every particle, and every cell is related to all the rest and is intrinsic to life. Every thought we think and every gesture we make is part of us. The degree to which we bring consciousness to these details is the degree to which we can live fully in every moment. How we relate with each detail seems to affect our sense of happiness and freedom. Practice and training remind us that we can develop the ability to meet each moment without judging and comparing. We can relate to the moment in its richness and its texture. We can take delight in the unfolding process.

## MAGIC IS PRACTICE

The principles of aikido are about cultivating the awareness that, as O'Sensei's says, "Love is the guardian deity of everything."[2] Maintaining our awareness of love is no easy task when we are faced with aggression or loss. Still, we know that it is possible because there are role models, men and women such as O'Sensei, Gandhi, and Mother Teresa, who opened their hearts and used love to transform hatred. One thing they shared was complete commitment: they were 100 percent lined up with this view of life. There was no hint of doubt, there was no fearful contraction of any kind. They were able to unify themselves completely with their belief, and we can do the same. Throughout the spiritual texts, the message is clear: the enemy is within. It is the inner conflicts and divisions that obscure our happiness. The message that we can find the way to peace and happiness is just as clear: we must face and resolve our inner conflicts.

O'Sensei says, "The 'Way' means to be one with the Will of God and practice it. If we are even slightly apart from it, it is no longer the

Way."[3] I was once at a seminar taught by Kisshomaru Ueshiba, O'Sensei's son, where he made a similar statement. He said, "The Way is paper thin, and if you are even one paper thinness off, it is no longer the Way."[4] This reminds me of a comment J. Krishnamurti once made, that you cannot be sort of free; it is like being sort of pregnant, impossible. What is inspirational about this view is the idea that we must make a total commitment to the cultivation of the Way.

It is like the song "The Hokey Pokey." At first, the song commands you to put different parts of your body into the circle: first your right arm and then later your left foot. Finally, you are asked to put your whole self in. Even in this silly dance, there is an exhilaration in the experience of using the whole body, the whole self. In the practice of aikido, when we can focus our energy completely, there is a sense of satisfaction and happiness that is palpable to both the giver and the receiver.

Cultivating the ability to be completely relaxed and focused, to bring resolution to our inner conflicts, is a process of self-development. When we encounter people who have this ability, there seems to be something extraordinary, something magical about them. They seem to be able to do difficult things easily. They have learned to move their experience from the plane of the ideal to the plane of the actual. The Way is simple, but it is not easy. Houdini describes it perfectly: "Magic is practice."[5] Or, as O'Sensei says, "This is not mere theory. You practice it. Then you will accept the great power of oneness with Nature."[6]

## INSPIRATION AND COMMITMENT

Inspiration and commitment are two important components of personal growth. The inspiration to walk the path can come from many places. Perhaps we become inspired because we have seen spiritual wealth and recognized the interplay of all things, we wish to live in accordance with these principles. Our progress will not always be easy. Spiritual and religious teachings mention temptations, which can draw us off our track. But at some point, we understand that we are seeking stillness, unconditional love, and the happiness that comes from accepting things as they are. Commitment is our metaphorical backbone: it is what allows us to make our journey. And to keep commitment strong in this world of temptation, we need to practice.

When I first observed aikido practice, I felt intuitively that it held the potential for healing my unhappiness. The philosophy that love is larger than an emotional attachment between two people, that all things are one, and that these truths can be used to turn away aggression was inspiration enough to set me on the path of O'Sensei's vision. And, indeed, my time on the path has cured me of much of my unhappiness.

Whatever we put our attention on grows. When we grasp this truth, we can take responsibility for how we live our lives. Our longing for our true home can be our inspiration. It can help us find, as Paul the Apostle writes in his letter to the Philippians (Phil. 4:7), "the peace of God, which passeth all understanding."[7] Each moment is a wealth of love and of intricate detail, of which we are an intrinsic part. This is our real home, our freedom, and our birthright of happiness.

## SERVICE

In my search for happiness, I began to wonder, *Who are the people who are really happy?* I found that some people say that they are basically happy, but this seems to be a partial truth. The ones who seem genuinely happy have a radiance about them. Their eyes seem to glow with light from within, and qualities of love and acceptance are palpable. I found that, without fail, these people lead lives that are, at their core, lives of service.

Albert Schweitzer says this on the subject of service: "I do not know what your destiny will be, but the one thing I know: the only ones among you who will be really happy are those who have sought and found how to serve."[8]

It is hard to talk about service without addressing giving and receiving. To serve is to give. As we give, that which we give moves through us to the recipient of our giving. If we are taking care of someone and treat that someone with respect, then we also feel the respect—the sensation of respect—that we are giving, for we cannot give what we do not have. In order to truly give something, we must feel the sensation of what we are giving. So in this sense, giving contains receiving.

Furthermore, in order to serve, there has to be something that receives that which is given. Giving and receiving work together. Both are needed in order to fulfill the cycle. Both are needed if a feeling of satisfaction or completeness is to occur. To receive with grace is also an aspect of service. It allows the giver to complete his or her mission or task; it serves life's cycle of movement and communication.

Aikido allows us to study giving through the body. During practice, we throw each other four times each. I give my body when I am in the role of the *uke*, the attacker. It is the initial generosity of the *uke* that allows the exchange between the two partners to take place. I serve my partner in this way so that he or she can refine the principles of balance, timing, and relaxation. I throw my partner four times, and then the favor is returned. We give each other the gift of a situation through which we can grow and develop.

The aikido dojo is a center where we come together as a community to serve one anther under the guidance of the teachers, who are responding to a tradition that believes in the ecumenical nature of the practice. The urge toward service is a natural outcome of love. How wonderful that so many people love to come to dojos and training places to practice! This shows that people want to find an empowering way to learn to serve.

Serving is not just taking care of someone: it is an attitude of care and respect that we can be bring to any part of our lives. Our willingness to serve is the foundation upon which virtues like compassion, loyalty, honor, and humility are developed. When our lives are occupied with the spirit of gratitude and generosity, the presence that we bring to each task is positive. Our commitment to service gives us a clear and steady view so that we are not impeded by the confusion of doubt. If, whatever we do, we do it in the spirit of service, a natural sense of meaning enhances our lives.

Mother Teresa had many wonderful sayings, but the one on her personal calling card was a summation of her approach:

The fruit of Silence is Prayer
The fruit of Prayer is Faith
The fruit of Faith is Love
The fruit of Love is Service
The fruit of Service is Peace.[9]

In her personal life, she relentlessly practiced these ideas until she became them. In service, our conflicts can find reconciliation, for service is not based on comparison: rather, it is founded on qualities such as respect and sympathetic joy.

In contrast, comparison opens the door to judgment, which is the great impediment to our happiness and capacity for service. It is important that we do not judge ourselves as better than or worse than anyone else. When we serve people less fortunate than ourselves, we can empathize with them that, for the moment, we are not in their position. Still, we need to understand that we are not immune to misfortune. That awareness keeps us from feeling so separate, while allowing us to be thankful that we can help.

In return, those to whom we are providing a service allow us to feel that we are useful; that we are doing something decent and can therefore have some appreciation for ourselves; that we are doing our part for the whole. This sense of appreciation and self-respect is the gift that those whom we serve give to us.

During my years at the women's prison, I was always touched to hear the volunteers say that the time they spent volunteering, giving their time in service, were often the happiest hours of their week. This kind of appreciation keeps us from comparing ourselves with others; instead, we become grateful that we can give ourselves in a way that is helpful.

An attitude of service provides us with both confidence and humility. Confidence gives us an expansive, willing quality; humility softens and opens our hearts. Together, they create a balance between the positive and the receptive. When we achieve this balance, our souls are satisfied. Greed and spiritual impoverishment give way to tolerance, dignity, and compassion: the foundation of a life that is led in accordance with the Way.

## LOVE

My friend Terry Dobson was the only person from the United States who apprenticed with O'Sensei during his last years. Terry spoke fluent Japanese and for a number of years he was a personal assistant to O'Sensei during his travels. I asked Terry what O'Sensei talked about both on and off the mat. I think that I was looking for some secret that would enlighten me as to how to use the shapes of the circle, square, and triangle more effectively, or how to direct the movements into specific spirals to make a more perfect technique. Terry said, "All he ever talked about was love, love, love, and more love."[10]

In the world of duality, love has an object or an objective. In the world of unity, love has no object to which to attach itself. As we mature spiritually, we begin to detach from grasping objects of love and begin to allow love based on an inner awareness of universal harmony to flow through us unimpeded. When I am aware of the interdependence of all things, I realize that it is ridiculous to love one thing and not another. Love for one thing need not be exclusive: it can increase our love for the world. When unconditional love is present, a quality of luminosity radiates equally in all directions.

This is the light that I perceive in those who are truly happy. This happiness does not depend on the fact that a person's love is returned by a particular person. Again, the Tao says it with poetic precision in verse 28:

Know the personal,
yet keep to the impersonal:
accept the world as it is.
If you accept the world,
the Tao will be luminous inside of you
and you will return to your primal self.[11]

When we experience life in terms of unity, there is no need for us to be acknowledged by another. It is only when a sense of duality arises that we experience life more in terms of this and that, me and you, self and other. If our feelings of love and happiness depend on another, then we will never be free. Yet it is difficult to detach from our personal experiences without retracting our feelings and our spirit. Through a process of self-cultivation, we can strengthen our ability to love without grasping, to detach without retracting. We must be willing to notice how our attention goes out and begins to attach to a person or thing. We must also train it to return to a state of unity that includes the person or thing.

In *The Method of Zen,* Eugen Herrigel writes,

This love, which can neither be disappointed nor encouraged from without, in which goodness, compassion, and gratitude are mingled, which does not woo, does not obtrude itself, make demands, disquieten, or persecute, which does not give in order to take, possesses astounding power, precisely because it shuns all power.[12]

Unity comes from within and without simultaneously, and is expansive and reflective in its nature. In order to uncover this unity as a reference point for our lives, we must trace our experience back and find the source of the radiance that brings light to the whole universe. It takes spirit and vitality to strengthen our commitment to wake up and remember the radiant essence. We must go beyond thinking, beyond the rational mind based on duality, to a state of Being. Born out of stillness, this is the state that fosters unconditional love. When we are filled with this love, there is happiness. When there is happiness, we are free.

This happiness is not just an absence of pain. It is inner state of grace that radiates no matter how much pain we are in or how difficult our circumstances are. It is a condition beyond the opposites of pleasure and pain. We can give this to ourselves, but we must be willing to commit to the path of rediscovering that radiant love that is at our core. What we can discover is a Self that includes all things and is, at the same time, nothing but openness and wonder.

Unity and multiplicity can coexist within our consciousness if we are able to cultivate a wide enough perspective to include them. We may have a sudden experience of this state, but it is our volition, our focused consciousness, that maintains a connection with this unity until it becomes as natural to us as walking or breathing.

It is easy to forget where the basis of true happiness lies and believe that certain achievements or relationships will supply us with what we think we long for. Once our awareness begins speeding, racing toward what we think will end our restlessness or uneasiness, it will lead us out of the present into the future or the past, both of which are projections. Projections are merely shadows dancing on the walls of our cave. It takes attentiveness to decelerate and return to the moment, to step out of our projections into the light of reality. We can develop the habit of waking up, we can stop speeding and notice our breath, the Earth, and the space around us and within us: we can become still. It is not our lack of something that causes our unhappiness: it is our separation from luminous emptiness, from stillness. As J. Krishnamurti writes, "There is a state of mind wholly, completely, alone; it is alone—not in isolation—alone in stillness and that stillness is beauty."[13]

Each moment is a new opportunity to touch the present with our awareness. We learn from experience that wanting things to be different than they are is suffering. Somehow we must find the strength, whether it comes from inspiration or longing, to end our suffering by turning our attention away from desires and fantasies of future happiness.

Mother Teresa says, "We are called upon not to be successful but to be faithful."[14] Faithful to what? Perhaps we can learn to be faithful to the present moment, to our breath, to our environment, or to the sensation of gravity that keeps us connected to the Earth. She also says, "We do no great things, only small things with great love."[15] Outside my door is a rock engraved with this saying. As I come and go from my house I am reminded that if I pay attention to what is around me, I can become sensitive to the "small things," the fluctuations and nuances that appear and disappear in a moment. Appreciation of the richness of the moment extinguishes our sense of impoverishment. Perhaps we will discover that what arises in its place is the practice of love, and this practice of love will set us free.

# AFTERWORD

The calligraphy for this book was created by my teacher, Mitsugi Saotome Shihan. His work is a visual teaching that can remind us of what it means to engage in the practice of freedom.

Saotome Sensei says, "The characters in the right-hand column are *shimpu o mote hito ni se su,* which signify 'spring wind carrying a warm feeling toward others.' They have the feeling of communication. On the left are *shin so omote mizu kara ima shi me ru,* which represent 'autumn frost; very clean and pure; look severely inside yourself.'

"This calligraphy carries the idea of the great responsibility of freedom, to take care of others and think of them first. It is very severe, not selfish."[1]

Sensei, *domo arigato gozaimashita.*

Wendy Palmer
Aikido of Tamalpais
Mill Valley, California
November 2001

# NOTES

## INTRODUCTION

1. There are various translations of Morihei Ueshiba's words, including "True *budo* is a work of love," in Kisshomaru Ueshiba, *Aikido* (Tokyo: Hozansha Publications, 1985), 179.

2. Lao Tzu, *The Way of Life: A New Translation of the Tao Te Ching,* trans. R. B. Blakney (New York: Mentor, 1983), verse 48, 101.

3. Ibid., verse 38, 91.

4. John Stevens, *Abundant Peace: The Biography of Morihei Ueshiba, Founder of Aikido* (Boston: Shambhala Publications, 1987), 33.

5. Morihei Ueshiba, quoted in Kisshomaru Ueshiba, *Aikido*, 177.

6. Mitsugi Saotome, *Aikido and the Harmony of Nature* (Shambhala Publications, 1993), 149.

7. Morihei Ueshiba, quoted in Kisshomaru Ueshiba, *Aikido,* 180.


## Part One: Initial Stages

### CHAPTER ONE: ANARCHY

1. *The American Heritage Dictionary*, 2d college ed., s.v. "anarchy."

2. Albert Einstein, quoted in Stephen Mitchell, *The Enlightened Mind: An Anthology of Sacred Prose* (New York: HarperPerennial, 1993), 191–92.

3. Anne Frank, *The Diary of a Young Girl*, trans. B. M. Mooyaart-Doubleday (New York: The Modern Library, 1952), 278.

4. Pema Chödrön, *Start Where You Are: A Guide to Compassionate Living* (Boston: Shambhala Publications, 1994), 4.

5. *The American Heritage Dictionary*, 2d college ed., s.v. "impoverish."

## CHAPTER TWO: ETIQUETTE

1. Stanley Pranin, "Etiquette and the Preservation of Well-Being," *Aikido Journal* 113, vol. 25, no. 1 (1998): 3.

2. J. Krishnamurti, *Freedom from the Known*, ed. Mary Lutyens (San Francisco: HarperSanFrancisco, 1969), 121.

3. Erich Fromm, *Escape from Freedom* (New York: Avon Books, Discus Books, 1970), 51.

4. Ibid., 57, 58.

5. Fyodor Dostoyevsky, *The Brothers Karamazov*, trans. Constance Garnett (New York: Dell Publishing, 1960), 187.

6. Ibid., 189, 190.

## CHAPTER THREE: MORALITY

1. Morihei Ueshiba, quoted in Kisshomaru Ueshiba, *Aikido*, 179.

2. Plato, *The Republic of Plato*, trans. Francis MacDonald Cornford (New York: Oxford University Press, 1945), 232.

3. *The American Heritage Dictionary*, 2d college ed., s.v. "fear."

4. Franz E. Winkler, M.D., *The Psychology of Leadership* (New York: The Myrin Institute, 1957), 25.

5. *The American Heritage Dictionary*, 2d college ed., s.v. "responsible."

6. Ibid.

## CHAPTER FOUR: COMPASSION

1. Morihei Ueshiba, quoted in Kisshomaru Ueshiba, *Aikido*, 178.

2. *The American Heritage Dictionary*, 2d college ed., s.v. "compassion."

3. Hazrat Inayat Khan, *The Complete Sayings of Hazrat Inayat Khan* (New Lebanon, N.Y.: Omega Publications, 1991), 128.

4. Morihei Ueshiba, quoted in Kisshomaru Ueshiba, *Aikido,* 178.

5. Nelson Mandela, quoted by a tour guide at Robben Island, South Africa, March 1997.

6. Brian Schwimm, *The Universe Is a Green Dragon: A Cosmic Creation Story* (Santa Fe, N.M.: Bear and Co., 1988).

7. Chögyam Trungpa, *Cutting Through Spiritual Materialism*, ed. John Baker and Marvin Casper (Boston: Shambhala Publications, 1987), 208.

8. Sharon Salsberg, *Lovingkindness: The Revolutionary Art of Happiness* (Boston: Shambhala Publications, 1997).

9. St. Francis of Assisi, "Prayer of St. Francis," quoted in Raghu Rai and Navin Chawla, *Faith and Compassion: The Life and Work of Mother Teresa* (Rockport, Mass.: Element Books, 1996), 185.


## Section Two: Refinement

## CHAPTER FIVE: CULTIVATING VIRTUE: INNER STILLNESS

1. Saotome Sensei, conversation with author, Satasota, Fla., December 1998.

2. Takeda Sensei, conversation with author, Yokohama, Japan, September 1997.

3. Morihei Ueshiba, quoted in Mitsugi Saotome, *Aikido and the Harmony of Nature*, 154.

4. Saotome Sensei, conversation with author, Aikido of Tamalpais, Mill Valley, Calif., 1987.

5. William Johnston, *The Still Point: Reflections on Zen and Christian Mysticism* (New York: Fordham University Press, 1995), 105.

6. Taisen Deshimaru, *The Zen Way to the Martial Arts,* trans. Nancy Amphoux (New York: E.P. Dutton, 1982), 48.

7. Albert Einstein, *The World as I See It,* trans. Alan Harris (New York: Citadel Press, 1993), 21.


## CHAPTER SIX: CULTIVATING THE WAY: SURRENDER

1. *The American Heritage Dictionary,* 2d college ed., s.v. "surrender."

2. Albert Einstein, quoted in Mitchell, *The Enlightened Mind,* 191.

3. Ibid.

4. Saotome Sensei, conversation with author, Sarasota, Fla., December 1998.

5. Ibid.

6. Lao Tzu, quoted in Stephen Mitchaell, *Tao Te Ching,* (HarperPerennial, 1988), verse 36, 36.

7. Ibid., verse 33, 33.


## CHAPTER SEVEN:
## THE OPEN DOOR TO FREEDOM: NONRESISTANCE

1. Morihei Ueshiba, quoted in Kisshomaru Ueshiba, *Aikido,* 180.

2. *The American Heritage Dictionary*, 2d college ed., s.v. "nonresistance."

3. Martin Luther King, Jr., *The Trumpet of Conscience* (New York: Harper and Row, 1967), 74, 75.

4. John Stevens, *The Secrets of Aikido* (Boston: Shambhala Publications, 1995), 104.

5. Chuang Tzu, "Cutting Up an Ox," quoted in Thomas Merton, *The Way of Chuang Tzu,* (New York: New Directions Books, 1969), 45–47.

6. Eknath Easwaran, trans., *The Bhagavad Gita,* (Tomales, Calif.: Nilgiri Press, 1985), verses 2–3, 196.

## CHAPTER EIGHT: TIME, SPACE, AND ENERGY

1. Chuang Tzu, quoted in Merton, *The Way of Chuang Tzu,* 47.

## CHAPTER NINE: UNDERSTANDING THE VERTICAL

1. Johnston, *The Still Point,* 98.

2. Ibid., 109.

## *Part Three: Fruition*

### CHAPTER TEN: FREEDOM

1. Peace Pilgrim, *Steps Toward Inner Peace: Harmonious Principles for Human Living* (Santa Fe, N.M.: Ocean Tree Books, 1993), 36.

2. Donn F. Draeger, *Classical Budo,* vol.2, *The Martial Arts and Ways of Japan Series,* (New York: Weatherhill, 1996), 34.

3. Nelson Mandela, *Long Walk to Freedom: The Autobiography of Nelson Mandela* (New York: Little, Brown and Company, 1995), 625.

4. Swami Rudrananda (Rudi), *Rudi: Spiritual Cannibalism,* 3d ed. (Cambridge, Mass.: Rudra Press, 1990), 65.

5. Lao Tzu, quoted in Brian Walker, *Hua Hu Ching: The Unknown Teachings of Lao Tzu,* trans. Brian Walker, (San Francisco: HarperSanFrancisco, 1995), 90.

6. Hiroshi Ikeda Sensei, conversation with author, San Raphael, Calif., March 1998.

7. J. Krishnamurti, *Freedom, Love, and Action* (Boston: Shambhala Publications, 1994), 35.

8. Lao Tzu, quoted in Blakney, *The Way of Life,* verse 11, 63.

9. Nicola Geiger, conversation with author, Santa Cruz, Calif., June 1999.

10. Hiroshi Ikeda Sensei, conversation with author, Mill Valley, Calif., March 1997.

11. Mandela, *Long Walk to Freedom,* 625.

12. June Jones, conversation with author, Port Elizabeth, South Africa, March, 1997.

13. Saotome Sensei, conversation with author, Sarasota, Fla., December, 1998.

14. Nicola Geiger, interview.

15. His Holiness, The Dalai Lama of Tibet, *The Way to Freedom,* ed. Donald S. Lopez, Jr. (San Francisco: HarperSanFrancisco, 1994), 1.

## CHAPTER ELEVEN: THE WAY: SELF-CULTIVATION

1. Morihei Ueshiba, quoted in Kisshomaru Ueshiba, *Aikido,* 178.

2. Ibid., 179.

3. Ibid., 180.

4. Kisshomaru Ueshiba, aikido seminar, Redwood City, Calif., 1980.

5. Harry Houdini, quoted in Ed Spielman, *The Spiritual Journey of Joseph L. Greenstein, the Mighty Atom: World's Strongest Man,* 2d ed. (Cobb, Calif.: First Glance Books, 1998), 223.

6. Morihei Ueshiba, quoted in Kisshomaru Ueshiba, *Aikido,* 178.

7. Phil. 4:7 Authorized (King James) Version.

8. For information about the work of Albert Schweitzer, contact The Albert Schweitzer Fellowship, 330 Brookline Ave., Boston, MA 02215; (617) 667–5111, www.schweitzerfellowship.org.

9. Rai and Chawla, *Faith and Compassion,* 19.

10. Terry Dobson, conversation with author, 1981. To read his stories about aikido, see Terry Dobson, *It's a Lot Like Dancing: An Aikido Journey,* ed.

Riki Moss, photography by Jan E. Watson (Berkeley, Calif.: Frog, Ltd., 1993).

11. Lao Tzu, quoted in Mitchell, *Tao Te Ching,* verse 28, 28.

12. Eugen Herrigel, *The Method of Zen,* ed. Hermann Tausend, trans. R. F. C. Hull (New York: Vintage Books, 1974), 95.

13. Krishnamurti, *Freedom from the Known,* 91.

14. Rai and Chawla, *Faith and Compassion,* 188.

15. Ibid., 158.

## AFTERWORD

1. Saotome Sensei, letter to author, 22 February 2001.

# APPRECIATIONS

Grateful acknowledgment is made to the following for permission to reprint previously published material:

Aikido Journal: Excerpts from "Etiquette and the Preservation of Well-Being" by Stanley Pranin, in *Aikido Journal* 113. Copyright © 1997 by Aiki News. Reprinted by permission of *Aikido Journal*, www.aikidojournal.com.

Faber and Faber: Excerpt from "Burnt Norton" in *Four Quartets* by T. S. Eliot. Copyright © 1936 and renewed 1964 by T. S. Eliot. Reprinted by permission of Faber and Faber Ltd., London.

Fordham University Press: Excerpts from *The Still Point: Reflections on Zen and Christian Mysticism* by William Johnston. Copyright © 1970 by Fordham University Press. Reprinted by permission of Fordham University Press.

Harcourt: Excerpt from "Burnt Norton" in *Four Quartets* by T. S. Eliot. Copyright © 1936 by Harcourt, Inc., and renewed 1964 by T. S. Eliot. Reprinted by permission of Harcourt, Inc.

HarperCollins: Quote from page 75 to be used as an epigraph, and excerpts from pages 91 and 121 from *Freedom from the Known* by Jiddu Krishnamurti. Copyright © 1969 by Krishnamurti Foundation Trust, Ltd. Reprinted by permission of HarperCollins Publishers, Inc.

HarperCollins: Excerpt from page 90, as submitted, from Hua Hu Ching: *The Unknown Teachings of Lao Tzu* by Brian Walker. Copyright © 1992 by

# ABOUT THE AUTHOR

Wendy Palmer, a sixth-degree black belt and cofounder of Aikido of Tamalpais, in Corte Madera, CA, has been teaching aikido since 1974. In 1980, she developed Conscious Embodiment, which uses aikido principles as a way to study boundaries, relationships, and leadership. She directed the Prison Integrated Health Program from 1990 to 1997. This is a volunteer project that provides classes in behavioral medicine at the Federal Correctional Institution in Dublin, California, and serves as a model for health promotion programs in prisons throughout the United States. She is the author of *The Intuitive Body: Aikido as a Clairsentient Practice* (North Atlantic Books, 2000), and teaches Conscious Embodiment in its companion video.

Correspondence to the author can be directed to:
Wendy Palmer, 809 Vendola Dr., San Rafael, CA 94903;
info@consciousembodiment.com.

For information about her Conscious Embodiment classes, as well as her books and video, visit www.consciousembodiment.com.

For information about her aikido classes, contact Aikido of Tamalpais, 142 Redwood Ave., Corte Madera, CA 94925; (415) 383–9474; www.tam-aikido.org.

# From the Publisher

Shambhala Publications is pleased to publish the Rodmell Press collection of books on yoga, Buddhism, and aikido. As was the aspiration of the founders of Rodmell Press, it is our hope that these books will help individuals develop a more skillful practice—one that brings peace to their daily lives and to the Earth.

To learn more, please visit www.shambhala.com.

# INDEX

accepting
  limitation, 17–18
  pain, 21
  who we are, 173–174
achievement, 23, 181
action, belief vs., 38
aikido
  aim of, 7–8, 115
  ambition in, 61–62
  black belt test, 47–48,
    160–161
  bowing in, 25, 43
  center when attacked and, 50
  Conscious Embodiment devel-
    oped from, 5–6
  as *do*, 4
  as etiquette, 33
  fear and practice of, 45–46
  heaven and Earth technique,
    146–147
  as internal practice, 114
  levels of study, 7
  love under pressure in, 6
  moral direction in, 37
  motto of, 117
  overview, 6–8

  as self-cultivation training,
    76–77
  sitting in stillness, 87–88
  Tao Te Ching and, 4
  timing in, 133
  for working with resistance,
    16–17
*Aikido Journal,* 25, 26
Aikido of Tamalpais, 2
ambition, 60–62
*American Heritage Dictionary, The*
  *anarchy* defined in, 11
  *compassion* defined in, 56
  *fear* defined in, 45
  *impoverish* defined in, 21
  *nonresistance* defined in, 115
  *responsible* defined in, 50
  *surrender* defined in, 97
anarchy, 11–24
  accepting limitations, 17–18
  achievement as sabotage, 23
  defined, 11
  in early life, 11–12
  experiencing resistance, 16–17
  impoverishment vs. the larger
    view, 21–23

2 1982 02943 3384

CPSIA information can be obtained
at www.ICGtesting.com
Printed in the USA
LVHW111800220522
719429LV00004B/284